NEVER CAUGHT A CASE

by
Craig Brown

Craig Clifton Publishing LLC
Milwaukee, Wisconsin

First Edition

ISBN: 979-8-9931643-1-1

Printed in the United States of America

Craig Clifton Publishing LLC
Milwaukee, Wisconsin
Craigbrown1215@yahoo.com

INTRODUCTION

Young Craig in Highland/Apollo Village 1980's

Just like my song says, "I ain't never caught a case". I'm proud to say I never been caught up in the system in ANY type of way. When I mention "the system," I'm talking about the network of institutions established by the U.S. government to regulate and control people in this country (mainly black people)—law enforcement, the military, the judiciary, the media, religion, financial institutions, and intelligence agencies. And by intelligence agencies, I don't just mean the C.I.A. or F.B.I.; I'm also referring to the informants and snitches on the streets who work with law enforcement daily. Also, The Mayor, Governor, Council men & women, Judges, CEO's, Employers, Company board of directors, Bank managers, Fire Chief, County Executive, Aldermen and Alderwomen, Prosecutors, Attorney General, District Attorney, Sheriffs, Police Captain, Senators, plants, wanna be influencers, and hand-picked so called local celebrities around the city. I believe they are all part of "the system".

These institutions were intentionally designed as mechanisms of control—ones that have historically benefited most white people while being weaponized against most Black people in every state simultaneously. This is also why in the federal court system, over 90% of the people they charge with something are convicted.

I never caught a case—I wish I could say it was because I was perfect and never went against these so-called laws, but that wouldn't be true. The truth is I learned about many of these systemic traps from first-hand experience at an early age. The first thing my loved ones taught me was don't trust nobody. It sounds like a cold thing to say to a minor right? Then as I got older, the more life started validating everything they said to me. I had to learn how to be realistic and see people for who they really were. And I had to learn how to predict the outcomes, and consequences of dealing with those types of people, or the outcomes and consequences of being in certain environments too much. This is the part of the game nobody can teach you. Either you have it, or you don't.

It wouldn't surprise me if about Ninety-Five percent of people I encounter are working with the system in some form or another. Some are doing the devils work intentionally, while others do unintentionally. Either way, my ability to trust most people is set at five percent.

Growing up in the projects, I never thought about the societal forces working against black people. I just knew something was making our people move wrong. The advice from my loved ones helped me stay clear of deception. I could end this book right here and what you just read would be worth the price you paid for it, but I will give you all of the details, bear with me.

This book isn't about shaming Black men and women who've caught charges, and it's not about bragging over things I may have done in the streets and how I ducked charges. My purpose is to highlight something that often goes uncelebrated: being a Black man in America with no criminal record is a GREAT thing.

I think it's corny when some dudes be out here acting like they are proud over having done time in jail or prison. Some even have the mentality that prison somehow makes them tougher than someone who never went. That mindset is so silly. Even more silly are those who actually believe that. In my opinion, it's harder to stay on the streets every day, avoiding the traps and temptations that are always present. That takes real strength and discipline.

I have deep respect for the brothers and sisters who've never been to jail or prison. In my opinion, it doesn't mean they were soft or weak. It doesn't mean that they never got involved in some of the things that goes on in the streets—it could mean they had the wisdom to see the traps and the understanding to move differently. At the same time, I respect those who've been locked up and came back honest about how harsh prison life really is. I respect the ones who return home, handle their business, and never go back.

Shoutout to the real ones doing time for good reasons—those who stood up to protect, educate, or provide for their families. If you were framed, hit with bogus charges, or made a mistake and you're working to bounce back from it, I wish you peace until you're free. But beyond all that, let's be clear: prison is no place for Black men or women.

Me being 100, I agree that we need laws, but the laws need to be fair across the board for everyone. However, it seems like this is not the case. These old, outdated laws were made by white people for the protection of white people, and this is where it gets shaky. It bothers me how white people feel they have the right to create laws to lock up black people after all the things they did in the past and continue to do to us to this day.

In the Holy Qur'an, Chapter 83, Al-Tatfif, verses 7-9 state: "Nay, surely the record of the wicked is in prison. And what will make thee know what the prison is? It is a written book." Maulana Muhammad Ali interprets this as a record of one's actions, where the deeds of wrongdoers are preserved, symbolizing a prison that restrains their ability to do good, ultimately hindering their progress.

When the Holy Qur'an says, "the wicked", I believe it describes whoever is calling the shots for the US government, and the White House. They are the wicked ones. Their record of wickedness and privilege over black people in America is not a display of real power and superiority like they think it is. Reality is, they are only creating a spiritual prison for themselves through their wicked deeds. These law makers are constantly creating worldly positions of power for themselves. And if you can only look at it from their small lens, it looks like they are superior. But ultimately their outcome will be a self-destructive journey towards spiritual confinement. They just can't see past their own greed and wickedness.

These devils believe that using whatever authority they have at the moment to block freedom, justice, and equality for all people is the way to go. Yet, they don't realize how their selfish desires for white privilege and white supremacy has restrained their ability to do good at the spiritual level. Those who implement systems and laws for the US Government are historical wrong doers. The record of their wicked deeds, and wrong doings are preserved in a book with God. The city may keep our people on CCAP, but God got the wicked whites on his CCAP.

If you're from Milwaukee, you know you don't have to do anything wrong to get caught up in this city. The whole system was designed by white people, for white people. Every chance they get they will use the system to their advantage. This is why the scale of justice is never equally balanced.

The city of Milwaukee was founded in 1846, but the constitution was drafted in 1787. Gouverneur Morris was the primary author of the constitution, and the articles of the confederation, and he also owned slaves. Therefore, anything he ever written is tainted with slave owner energy.

Fast forward to modern day times, and the energy is the same. Traffic stops are excessive, profiling is nonstop, and avoiding jail in this city feels like a full-time job. Milwaukee is one of the most segregated cities in America for a reason—I believe it's because the courts need cases, the police need arrests, and the state needs free labor. They have perfected ways to lure black people into their systemic traps.

This book is about how I never fell into those traps despite the system being built to work against people like me. I have relatives and friends that are still doing prison time, and I regularly get collect calls from them asking me to send them money. As long as they weren't locked up for something predatory like pedophile charges, then I always send them money, imagining they'd do the same for me.

I remember when I bought my first decent trapper with my own money. It was a blue 1985 Grand Marquis. I was probably in my late teens. My mechanic was a dope fiend, but he did good work on cars. No matter the weather—too hot outside, rain, snow, freezing cold, dark—he didn't care. He would come and work on my car if I paid him to. One day, while working on the Marquis he said, "I think every black man should go to jail at least once in his life, at least for a day." I didn't say anything, but I remember thinking, yeah, that rock he just smoke got him tripping. His words stuck with me for many years, because I didn't want to find out what it would be like to spend 1 day in jail.

I wasn't like Big Meech in these streets,...well actually, I wasn't even like little Meech either. At least he played a character version of a big-time drug dealer on a TV series. It doesn't take away from the fact that I have my own unique experiences with the street life. There was a time in my life I was involved in some things that could've gotten me incarcerated. My experience in those things is what makes my book valid. I don't know how to write about things unless I really did it. However, those things will not be the main focus of this book.

Once I learned about the concepts of the 5% NGE it stuck with me. I still believe that 85% of the people I encounter are "deaf, dumb, and blind," and lack knowledge of self. Many people that I met in the streets were smart when it came to some things, but they were "deaf, dumb, and blind" when it came to understanding how the system worked against us. It is also possible that they knew the system too and just didn't care. All they seen was a chance to make fast money, and they accepted whatever risks came with that.

As far as the girls I liked, it didn't matter to me how fine they were I was never going to go above and beyond to try to impress them. I wasn't going to tell them my business or anyone else's. I stayed cool with everyone, but I kept my distance when I needed to.

In the hood somebody will always want something from you. You must know how to say no. You must know how to control your emotions and not get caught up in other people's wants. You must put your best interests first, and be ok with telling people no.

Sometimes other people's wants will get you caught up in other people's drama. That's what much of this book is about. If you know deep down that a particular situation isn't for you, stay clear. Don't let your environment push you into situations that could cost you your freedom or life over senseless drama.

When my dope fiend mechanic buddy made that comment about all black men should go to jail at least 1 day, I think he was really saying that in Milwaukee, black people should know that we are targeted. We are always one step away from getting locked up for something. Sometimes it doesn't matter if we didn't do anything wrong. Just stay prepared. If that is what he meant, then I can agree with that. Milwaukee's local law enforcement will keep you on their radar all day everyday.

Milwaukee has about 77,000 streetlights and 10,000 alley lights. If those lights could talk, they'd tell some wild stories. But none of them would shine on police brutality or racial injustice against black people. My book will focus on these things.

I know some people—especially MAGA white folks and the black ones trying to be in their good graces and always parroting what white MAGA says—will have a problem with this book. I don't care. I will always represent for those who were promised 40 acres and a Mule. Never forget, the 14th Amendment is for black people, and reparations are overdue.

Chapter 2 will break down the statistics—the employment, education, and wealth gaps that were likely created by design. Poverty breeds desperation, and desperation leads to bad decisions. Bad decisions could lead to incarceration.

Chapter 3 is about my mom. She taught me to stand alone, to put family first, and to trust in God. That foundation kept me focused when it was time for me to jump off the porch and be in these streets fully responsible and accountable for myself.

Chapter 4 is about my older siblings. My brothers taught me about the streets—what to do and what not to do. My sister taught me what to look for in women. They are all at least ten years older than me, so I had the advantage of learning from their mistakes before I got to their age.

Chapter 5 is about my neighborhood—Highland Park Projects. We moved like a family, and most dudes around me were about getting money. I respected that. They were a little older than me, and I learned by watching them the same way I watch my own brothers. At the same time, my younger friends started coming up, and they inspire me too. Most of us are all still friends till this day. Our neighborhood was still caught up in the system though.

Chapter 6 is about Milwaukee, a city considered to be one of the most segregated in the nation. Milwaukee's Black communities face systemic barriers that keep us trapped in a cycle of struggle—high unemployment, high incarceration, gun violence is high, and people drink, and smoke whatever to get high. The system is designed to keep us dependent, distracted, and disenfranchised, ensuring that we remain stagnant instead of rising above. Again, every time I mention "the system," I'm referring to the network or web of institutions the U.S. government put in place to work together to control people in this country (mainly black people)—The primary institutions are: the police, the military, the legal system, media, religion, financial institutions, and intelligence agencies. Not just the C.I.A or F.B.I, the intelligence agencies also include the snitches and confidential informants on the streets who cooperate with law enforcement daily. And what color are the people running the whole system? Mostly white if not all.

Chapter 7 is about my understanding of the Articles of the confederation, and the constitution, it was created by white people for white people to secure the Blessings of Liberty to themselves and their Posterity.

Chapter 8 is about my vision. I see a Milwaukee where we all understand these systemic traps and learn how to avoid them, where we support each other instead of hating, where we show up to vote out racist judges every spring, and where we hold people accountable—especially those who work in Milwaukee, profit off of our communities, and then run back to their suburban homes without giving anything back.

In Chapter 9 the conclusion, I want people to understand a Black man with no criminal record is a GREAT thing. I never caught a case, but that doesn't make me better than anybody else. I just knew I had to move differently, keep my faith in God, and know the system from the time it was created until now.

Who can write about how to stay out of prison better than someone who has never been there? Who can break down the achievement gaps in employment in Milwaukee better than someone who's worked at a major corporation for over 20 years? Who can expose the disparity in education better than someone who mentors youth and young adults daily? ME THAT'S WHO!!

Chapter 2

Statistics

My favorite rappers are Ice Cube, and Too Short, but I'm also a huge East Coast Hip Hop fan. Listening to artists like Nas, Rakim, King Sun, Poor Righteous Teachers, Brand Nubian, AZ, and Wu Tang Clan I learned a lot about the Supreme Mathematics. These MCs are considered among the best the East has to offer. These great artists inspired me to research more about my own history.

My favorite book of all time is Message to The Blackman in America by The Honorable Elijah Muhammad. I can read this book over and over. Let me be clear, I'm not a Muslim or 5% NGE, but I admire them a lot. To me The Supreme Mathematics means truth, because math only deals with facts. In Math your answer is either right or its wrong. You must keep working until the answer is right.

In this chapter, I strive to provide all relevant stats and numbers that explain what's going on with our people. In Wisconsin, where an estimated 364,000 Black people reside, 1 in every 36 black adults are in prison. Prisons are incentivized to stay full. Many private prison companies have contracts with the government. These profit-driven prisons can use their money and influence to lobby for harsher laws, pressure judges for longer sentences, and push policies that keep people behind bars.

As of this writing. In Wisconsin, black people make up just 6% of the state's population but account for 42% of its prison population. These numbers tell me that there is something going on systemically that is pushing for mass incarceration of black people. By applying Supreme Mathematic principles to our circumstances, we can better identify specific individuals and institutions that play a role in either perpetuating or dismantling these systems that push for mass incarceration.

According to Supreme Mathematics, the population can be divided into three distinct groups: the 85%, the 10%, and the 5%. The 85%, or the "deaf, dumb, and blind," are those who lack knowledge of self and are manipulated by systems designed to keep them down bad. If we apply this concept to Wisconsin's Black population, that would mean approximately 309,400 Black individuals are trapped in cycles of misinformation, systemic disenfranchisement, and miseducation, following narratives dictated by those who do not have their best interests at heart.

The 10%, representing those who have knowledge but use it for their own personal gain, amount to 36,400 Black individuals in Wisconsin. These are the sellouts, the wanna be influencers, the lame media personalities, snitches, and hand-picked so called local celebrities, who knowingly align themselves with oppressive systems created by white policy makers rather than working to dismantle them. They exist in positions of power, often within government, business, entertainment, and education, using their influence to maintain the status quo. They try to pass themselves off as spokespeople for you and me, but their real role is to ensure that most of us in Milwaukee never rise to our full potential.

That leaves the 5%, the solid ones, those who possess knowledge of self and work tirelessly to uplift the people. Applying the supreme mathematics to Wisconsin's Black population, only 18,200 people fall into this category statewide. However, when factoring in elders and children—those who may not be able to actively engage in leadership or direct activism—this number is probably cut in half to 9,100 individuals statewide, with possibly only 5,000 scattered around in Milwaukee trying to fight this system. Don't forget.

When I mention "the system," I'm referring to the entire network or web of institutions the U.S. government put in place to control (mainly black people) in this country—the police, the military, the legal system, media, religion, financial institutions, and intelligence agencies. Not just the C.I.A or F.B.I, this also includes the snitches and confidential informants on the streets who work with law enforcement daily. The good people are usually always outmanned, and out gunned, but that don't mean we should quit.

Milwaukee's black communities are more heavily policed than white neighborhoods. Black people in Milwaukee are more likely to be stopped, searched, and arrested than any other race of people. It is like a full-time job trying to stay out of jail. This information highlights the immense challenge at hand: how can such a small percentage of conscious minded individuals combat the forces of misinformation, oppression, and systemic issues that continue to harm our communities?

One of the most glaring examples of a systemic trap in Wisconsin is the state of education for Black students. In Milwaukee Public Schools (MPS), where roughly 38,000 students are enrolled, 49% have faced suspension in a single school year in 2023—these stats directly affect the development of our black youth. Black students in Milwaukee are suspended at nearly 4 times the rate of white students. Black youth are also five times more likely to be detained or committed to youth facilities than white youth. This is by design. This is not because white students are smarter or more well behaved than black students. Between August 2022 and August 2023, MPS recorded 15,229 suspensions, demonstrating the extent to which black children are criminalized from an early age.

For the 2023-2024 school year MPS recorded 18,438 suspensions for black students, and just 713 suspensions for white students. When kids are suspended from school, they will likely end up on the streets, and I'm sure those who are working behind the system are anticipating this. One in 36 Black adults in Wisconsin are already behind bars. When the state talks about renovating or building new prisons, they already have in mind how they will get more inmates by using "the streets" to keep all prison beds full.

When black youth are suspended from school, they are systemically funneled toward the street life, where they face increased risks of violence or incarceration. The school to prison pipeline is real. Regardless if black youth end up in juvenile detention or dead, the system profits from the loss. Either way, the system wins.

The suspensions are policies and practices upheld by white policy makers and supported by the 10%—those who are aware of the truth but choose to align with bogus systems rather than fight against them. It is our duty to help the 5% challenge these structures, to expose the deceit of the 10%, and to awaken the 85% to their true potential.

Leadership, in this sense, is not just about positional power—it is about community leadership, educational leadership, and grassroots activism. It requires us to reshape the narrative, advocate for policy changes, and create safe spaces where black youth can thrive without fear of systemic retaliation. We know that black people historically have been portrayed by police and the media in the worst way to justify their mistreatment, and misrepresentation of our people.

Understanding Supreme Mathematics in the context of community building allows us to see the real reasons why so many black children are failing, why our communities remain in a cycle of oppression, and why only a small fraction of us are truly fighting for improvement. If we do not take the lead, if we do not step up to challenge the system, then nothing will get better for us as a collective.

The two main things we can do to make changes immediately is knowing our rights and knowing how to apply supreme mathematics in all situations.

Knowledge (1) is the foundation—our youth and young adults must know their rights. One of the most effective ways to empower Black youth and young adults in Milwaukee is to educate them on their legal rights. Wisconsin's corrupt legal system thrives when black people do not know our rights, leading to unnecessary arrests, police encounters, and school disciplinary actions that derail futures.

By integrating Supreme Mathematics principles, we can use knowledge (1) and wisdom (2) to create understanding (3) and break free from the societal forces that entrap our community.

1. Rights When Dealing with Police

Right to Remain Silent (5th Amendment): We do not have to answer police questions beyond identifying ourselves. We should say: "I am invoking my right to remain silent."

Right to Refuse Searches (4th Amendment): If police ask to search you, your car, or your home, you can legally refuse unless there is a warrant or probable cause. We should say: "I do not consent to this search"

Right to Ask if They're Free to Leave: If stopped by police, we should ask: "Am I free to go?" If the answer is yes, we should get up out of there. If detained, we should ask: "Am I being arrested?"

Right to an Attorney (6th Amendment): If arrested, we should immediately request a lawyer and avoid speaking without legal representation.

2. Rights in Schools (MPS Students)

Right to Due Process: Students cannot be suspended or expelled without a formal hearing. They should demand a written explanation and appeal unfair discipline.

Right to Free Speech (1st Amendment): Students can express their views, including through protest, if it does not disrupt school functions.

Right Against Unreasonable Searches (4th Amendment): School officials need reasonable suspicion, not just a hunch, to search students 'backpacks or lockers.

Right to Fair Special Education Services: If a student is placed in special education unfairly, parents can demand proper evaluations and challenge the placement.

3. Rights When Stopped While Driving

Right to Remain Silent: Drivers only need to provide their license, registration, and proof of insurance. They do not have to answer additional questions.

Right to Refuse a Car Search: Police cannot search a vehicle without probable cause or the driver's consent. The proper response is: "I do not consent to a search."

Right to Record Police (1st Amendment): Individuals can legally record police interactions, if they do not interfere with law enforcement duties.

4. Rights Against Housing and Employment Discrimination

Fair Housing Rights: Landlords cannot deny housing based on race, gender, or having a criminal record.

Right to Equal Employment Opportunity: Employers cannot discriminate based on race, and Milwaukee prohibits employers from asking about criminal records early in the hiring process.

5. Rights When Protesting

Right to Peacefully Assemble (1st Amendment): Public protests are legal as long as they follow city laws regarding time and location.

Right to Record Public Officials: Protesters can film police or other officials as long as they do not interfere with law enforcement duties.

Right to Not Be Harassed for Protesting: Police cannot target individuals for participating in legal protests, though they can arrest people violating trespassing or vandalism laws.

By integrating the principles of Supreme Mathematics, we can use Knowledge (1) and Wisdom (2) to create Understanding (3)—the key to breaking free from the societal forces that entrap our communities. Knowledge is the foundation, but wisdom is the application. Knowing our rights is not enough; we must understand how to use them in real-life situations.

Understanding, the third principle, is the best part. It's the clarity that comes when our people recognize the direct connection between legal empowerment and the ability to navigate systemic traps.

Once we reach this level of consciousness, we begin to grow in culture and freedom. We refine our power, manifest true equality, and give all praises due to God (7).

From there, we can build (8) strategies that destroy barriers, and through Born (9)—the realization of new realities—we let knowledge come into being. That's what leads us to the Cipher (0), a state of wholeness, self-sufficiency, and true freedom.

If we shared these Supreme Mathematics principles throughout our communities and stay equipped with knowledge—particularly knowing our rights—we reclaim control of our narrative. This is how we uplift the 85%, the ones who've been left blind to systems designed to keep us down bad. Knowledge is the first step toward building a strong Black community in Milwaukee. Supreme knowledge will get us the freedom, justice, and equality we truly deserve.

Look at the statistics: disproportionate suspensions in schools, high arrest rates, severe economic disparities, and this low-down dirty system looks for ways to generate money off of it. This can't be all random—They counter spend money to block access to factual knowledge, and other resources. But when we educate and empower ourselves, we begin to reclaim our power. We set the stage for a generation that won't just survive—but thrive. The next generation will be proud of us for paving the way.

I believe Supreme Mathematics gives us the tools—not just to identify oppression—but to actively dismantle it. This is how we build a strong Black community in Milwaukee. We have to start with self-determination. This is another reason why I never caught a case. I utilize concepts like Supreme Mathematics. If someone asked me to do something that didn't add up, I had no problem saying no. If the math or the logic wasn't right, I wasn't doing it.

I'm grateful to hip hop that I learned about Supreme Mathematics and the Supreme Alphabets. My mom was Baptist. She didn't know anything about the 5% NGE, but she would probably refer to their teachings as just good common sense. The mathematics my mom taught me was the Ten Commandments. From early on, I was dealing with math in every form—whether in school, spiritual, or street.

My people taught me how to weigh certain products on a scale, and how to break it down by the ounce. They could have been mathematical geniuses how well they knew how to count grams. Everything makes sense when you break down that math of it. The system made it easy for us to see ourselves in certain characters they fed us through TV, Videos, Music, and all their other approved media outlets. Characters like Nino Brown, Bishop in Juice, or Kane and O-Dog in Menace II Society, Snowfall, Power, BMF gave us false representation of what life in the hood for most black men really looked like. The system uses their outlets to paint black men as if we were born violent—as if the system is not behind the scenes controlling and manipulating it all.

The truth? Gang life is far more complex than the media knows. Most of the gang members and dealers I know aren't just ignorant fools looking to rob and kill people like how the media show it in movies and rap videos. The people I know wanted to protect their community at all costs. They just didn't realize they weren't up against other dealers, and neighborhoods. The biggest rival to us is always the system. And how the system has the resources, and funds to take the toughest guys we know in our neighborhoods and turn them into informants.

As soon as you join a gang or sell drugs, you are one foot in the system. The longer you stay in that life, the more likely you will catch a case, or get murdered, or become an informant, and the system wins either way. That's the most accurate street mathematics.

I'm a proud 414 representative—raised on 20th and Juneau, Highland side. Over time, I learned about more than just the streets. I discovered people the system didn't make it easy for me to learn about: Marcus Garvey, Nat Turner, Wallace Fard Muhammad, the Honorable Elijah Muhammad, Malcolm X, Clarence 13X, Bobby Seale, Huey Newton, Fred Hampton, Rev. Dr. Martin Luther King Jr., Minister Louis Farrakhan, and Barack Obama. These are my heroes.

And the women? Just as powerful. I give honor to Harriet Tubman, Madam C.J. Walker, Fannie Lou Hamer, Oprah Winfrey, Queen Mother Moore, Zora Neale Hurston, Lauryn Hill, Sister Souljah, Queen Latifah, Angela Davis, Michelle Obama, Toni Momon, and the greatest woman I've ever known—my mother, Martha Brown.

*

Chapter 3

My Mom

Young CB and Moms 80's

My mother was the greatest woman I've ever known. I got a lot of my game from her. She taught me good old fashioned common sense. She taught me to look at people, situations, and information clearly. See it for what it is. She taught me about consequences. Think about what could happen before I make a move or give my opinion on any situation. In the heat of the moment is when I need to be able to make the best choices. This was advantageous to me because having common sense the way she raised me helped me keep my head on straight. She taught me about love. I learned from her to put my family first over everything else. And in an indirect way, she taught me how to pick the right woman for me. All excellent game, and I knew if I applied it right, I would never have to fear nothing or nobody in this world but God.

My mother was born in a small town right outside of Jackson, Mississippi in 1944. She moved to Chicago around 1956, and eventually made Milwaukee, Wisconsin her home around 1962. She loved Mississippi — she'd tell me all the time about her life growing up on a farm in the country outside of Jackson.

When mom was born in 1944. Franklin D. Roosevelt was President of the United States. It's important for me to mention who was POTUS and what their policies were at the time my mother and siblings were born. It allows me to give details about how these systems impacted my family's lives. People love to talk about how great FDR was, but if he was really that great, he would've acknowledged Jesse Owens as a national hero after winning four gold medals in the 1936 Olympics. That didn't happen. However, the hate crimes against black people did happen, every day with little to no media coverage. It's still traumatizing to me to this day.

The great depression started in 1929 and lasted until about 1941. There were no safety nets for the poor—just bailouts for the greedy white businessmen who caused the depression.

FDR, who served three terms—the longest of any U.S. president—oversaw a lot of progress, but not for Black people.

Toward the end of his presidency, FDR's running mate was Henry A. Wallace—a man the political establishment hated. Why? Because Wallace was against imperialism and he was openly non-racist. Wallace once said, "Superior ability is not the exclusive possession of any one race or class, provided men are given the right opportunities." He also said, "The future must bring equal wages for equal work regardless of sex or race." Statements like that made sure Wallace would never be allowed to lead. So, when FDR died in office, the racist political bosses of that time decided that Harry S. Truman would be the next President of the United

States. Truman was only a high school graduate, but he had the support of rich racist white men who thought anybody can be president inside their system.

Many decades later, my mom would celebrate Barack Obama's election without ever realizing the difference between Obama's and Truman's journeys. Truman didn't finish college and still made it to the White House. Obama had to graduate from Harvard and be near-perfect to get there.

By the time mom moved to Milwaukee, she lived through the Kennedy assassination in 1963. Lyndon B. Johnson became president, and during his presidency, both Malcolm X and Dr. Martin Luther King Jr. were assassinated. She lived through all of that.

My mom wasn't political. As far as politics go, when I got older, she told me to just vote Democrat. She believed Democrats mostly looked out for poor people. She told me the Republicans mostly look out for rich white people. I learned that Wall Street execs, and corporate lawyers—Shapes U.S Policies, and they are mostly republicans. Up against that system, I can see how my mom might have thought that her opinion or vote didn't matter. She might not have ever voted, but when I turned 18, she always told me to go vote....and I did. And I never voted Republican.

Through all the hate my mom may have seen growing up in the Jim Crow, and civil rights era, she never let it break her loving spirit. If anything, it only seemed to make her more devoted to loving her own family. It might be selfish of me to think this way, but I always appreciated that she never put a man before her kids. I never met my biological father, and I never had a stepdad. I don't know what happened in her life that made her swear off men, but personally, I was glad she did. I had brothers, uncles, and cousins who could guide me— good or bad, right or wrong. They taught me what it meant to be a man.

My mom stayed single. If you asked her, she would tell you she didn't want any of those no-good men, so she abstained. She wasn't into women either. I can speak for my brothers and sister that we all supported her decision. No man we knew of was good enough for our mom. That's why we were all so protective of her and made sure she gave her love to us. 100% of her emotional, and spiritual energy went to raising her children, and I'm a better man because of it.

My mom loved me. She loved me so much I never felt poor. Every woman I've dealt with on a serious level told me they could tell my mom spoiled me. I never

thought of it as being spoiled. To me, it was mom giving me the game and the confidence I needed so nobody could ever make a fool out of me.

For example, in elementary school, if a girl in my class called me fat, I would tell my mom when I got home. She would say stuff like, "Awe, that girl just likes you, don't pay her no attention." If it hadn't been for my mom's words, I probably would've reacted foolishly and back hand slap that girl. Then that would have got me suspended or expelled from school. But because my mom raised me to think before I act, I never let somebody's words get me out of character. She taught me don't fight girls. But if a boy tries to hit me, I better hit them back. Hit them as hard as I can.

As a preteen, my siblings sometimes talked about me like a dog. One of my older brothers used to rank on me all the time. He called me everything but a child of God—fat, musty, adopted (even though I wasn't.). He would talk about my bad acne, big head, and crooked teeth. Bro would not let up. Whenever my mom heard him talking about me, she would make him leave me alone. He'd tell her to stop babying me, and she'd say, "Well, HE IS my baby, leave him alone!!" If it wasn't for her love, my self-esteem could've been crushed. I probably would've tried to fight my almost-grown brother for ribbing me like that.

It wasn't just him. My cousins ranked on me too. Maybe they thought they were toughening me up. Or maybe they were jealous of how my mom loved me. Her love outweighed every insult that came my way. By the time I became a man, nothing could break my confidence. People could call me fat, big headed, stingy, selfish—it didn't matter. All I could hear was my mom's voice telling me, "Don't pay them silly folks no attention. Look at them, they don't have no business talking about nobody." And those three words, "look at them", helped me in so many situations. I'd look at them and decide, these haters don't deserve to be around a player like me. I only want those who love me to be in my presence. That was mom secret weapon. That's how she protected herself. It was also how she beat the system. Love was her currency, and she spent it wisely—on her children and her grandchildren. She didn't waste her love or energy on people who didn't deserve it. Now I'm the same way, I don't waste my love or energy on people who don't deserve it.

Growing up on welfare never really bothered me. When my mom sent me to the corner store on State Street with food stamps, I didn't feel ashamed. I knew she wasn't the type just sitting around waiting on a check. Even the Arabs who owned the store knew we weren't broke. In fact, we were one of the few families who could get stuff on credit from the store. At the time, I didn't even know what "credit" was.

I found out the hard way. One day, when I was about 9 or 10 yrs old. I went in the store and stole some cookies. They didn't yell at me, chase me, or even say a word. They just added it to my mom's tab—like, "Yeah, got eeem".

The store owner, Mario, was a fool. We called him "Al Pacino" because he looked like Scarface. He dressed and talked crazy like him too. He called my mom right away. By the time I got home, she already knew what I did. She was mad—mad in a "you embarrassed me" type of way, and that hurt me more than if she would have whoop me or put me on punishment.

She sent me back to the store to apologize. I was scared. I was thinking they might take me to the back of the store and pull out chainsaws on me. Just like the Columbians did to Scarface in the movie. Mario accepted my apology and said, "If it wasn't for your mom, I would've called the police." That's street credit. Lesson learned: I never stole nothing else again.

My mom always kept a hustle going. She ran her own candy store out of our apartment, selling chips, candy bars, sodas, and hot dogs to people in the projects. This was smart because sometimes people didn't feel like walking to the corner store, especially at night. Kids and adults came to our place all the time spending money. She also ran an in-home daycare, keeping kids while their parents worked. They paid her every week. On weekends, she hosted card games—"Pitty Pat" and "Tunk"—and took her cut for hosting. She sold Avon too. She would sell anything except her body. And all that hustle paid off. And she always made sure to spend a nice amount of her money on me.

When I went outside to play, she'd tell me, "Be careful." I knew what she meant: avoid situations where the police might get called. That was no small thing, because in the projects 90% of situations going on could've brought the police. This is where her lessons on common sense saved me. I paid attention to what people said and did around me. I thought about the consequences I would deal with before reacting. Most of the time, I made the right choice. But sometimes, people will bother you for no reason.

I remember in middle school, the principal pulled me out of class for no reason at all. He called my mom, questioning how a kid from the projects on free lunch could afford designer clothes. My mom snapped on him right over the phone, and he apologized. Years later, I learned that same principal caught a dope case, moving kilos. No wonder he was all in our business.

My mom always had my back. She seemed to know people would try to mistreat me, and she prepared me for it. She warned me about how deceptive and manipulative people could be.

No matter what my friends in Highland were doing, if my mom told me not to do something, nine times out of ten, I didn't do it. My friends respected her too. They used to make fun of me for having a 9 p.m. curfew. After nine was when the projects really got turnt up. Some would say I missed a lot of action in the jects, but I didn't feel like I missed anything. I was having fun at home, writing raps, playing Sega, Monopoly or Spades with my family, or listening to music.

My mom loved rap music too. MC Hammer, Heavy D, 2pac, and 50 Cent were her favorites.

Growing up, I saw weak-minded people get caught up in the streets. They may not have had nobody to tell them to go home, so they end up listening to the wrong people. My Auntie Ruby used to say, "See a fool, bump their head." That stuck with me. I was never going to be nobody's fool. My mom allowed me to make mistakes and learn from it, but she also gave me her thoughts on how I should avoid certain mistakes in the first place.

I learned at a young age that all street money wasn't good money. When my mom had card games at her house, if someone tried to come in drunk, she would not let them play. She would tell them they had to leave because she knew drunk money wasn't good money. All the women in my family were strong black women. My Auntie Jo was always fly. Ice stay dripping from her diamonds. She knew everybody in the projects, and everybody respected her. My Auntie Hyrticina was the leader of the family—whatever she said, her sisters listened. If I hadn't listened to my mom about the streets, I would have been dead or in prison back in the 90's. My mom wanted me to graduate college. That was the least I could do for her. In my opinion, school is easy. The streets are harder. College costs money, but the streets could cost your freedom or your life if you're in too deep. The streets are something different every day, and common sense told me I didn't need to be in the streets, NOT EVERY DAY. The decision was easy for me. I got that college degree like she told me to. I saw my mom get money in so many ways, and that hustle rubbed off on me. I knew the government was against me so relying on the government for help was never an option. I've owned a cleaning company, I worked at one of the biggest telecommunications companies in the world, done business consulting, owned rental properties, learned the stock market, started a nonprofit, and oh yeah, I use to rap too. I stay working and stay prayed up just like mom.

All praises due to God for my mom, Martha Brown—the greatest woman I've ever known.

Craig Brown

*

Chapter 4

My Big Brothers And My Sister

My Sis(late 80's-early 90's) & My Big Bro's(late 90's-early 2000's)

My siblings—DB (1963), Ty (1964), Kat (1965), and Stan (1966)—were born right in the thick of a war most people don't talk about. The war right here in America: a war of white people using the government, and its entire system to sustain their white privilege no matter who must suffer for it. My siblings were born during the years of John F. Kennedy, Lyndon B. Johnson, and Richard Nixon—a string of presidents who, despite their rhetoric, upheld and enforced systems designed to control black people and keep most of us broke and suffering.

This was the Civil Rights era. Black people were being attacked with fire hoses and police dogs just for demanding equal rights. While the images of brutality shocked the nation, most of the wickedness was being orchestrated behind closed doors in the white house. Even before my siblings were born, Dwight D. Eisenhower (1953–1961) served as president, but J. Edgar Hoover was really calling the shots. Hoover made accusations that the Civil Rights Movement was backed by communist. He feared an alliance between anti-war activists and civil rights groups. He launched COINTELPRO in 1956—a FBI program that illegally surveilled, infiltrated, and disrupted Black organizations and their allies. Eisenhower had to have known about what hoover was doing, and he still authorized it.

From 1956 to 1971, the FBI targeted Dr. Martin Luther King Jr., the Honorable Elijah Muhammad, the Nation of Islam, Huey Newton, the Black Panther Party—even the White Panther Party, a white anti-racist group. Anyone pushing back against systemic inequalities was labeled a threat. These illegal operations were backed at the highest levels of government, showing just how far the system would go to make sure the Blessings of Liberty remained for white people by white people.

By the time John F. Kennedy became president (1961–1963), there were small gestures of support—like when he called Coretta Scott King while MLK Jr. was in jail. Some say Kennedy wanted to move the country in a better place for all, but he was assassinated before we could find out. Lyndon B. Johnson became president (1963–1969), he promised "The Great Society" but his legacy to me is about the scandal he created in the Vietnam War.

It's important for me to mention who was POTUS and what their policies were at the time my siblings were born. It allows me to give details about how these systems directly impacted my family's lives.

This was the system my siblings were born into—a domestic war where any black resistance was criminalized, and leadership was either targeted or murdered. In Milwaukee, I don't think our single mothers were taught to defend against or identify systemic attacks on our family. Since they were not taught that, they fought in other ways like showing love, and nurturing those in our community. Survival was the main priority for our mothers. Then survival is what they taught to my siblings.

When Richard Nixon took office (1969–1974), he followed in Johnson's footsteps. Both resigned from their presidency, but the blood sucking of the poor continued. Nixon's infamous quote—"If the president does it, it's not illegal"—summed up his incompetence. His administration tried to spy on the Democratic Party, leading to the Watergate scandal. When Gerald Ford (1974–1977) became president, he gave Nixon a pardon for the Watergate scandal. From what I researched Ford didn't even like Nixon, but white people will stick together before doing anything that would jeopardize white privilege. Instead of jail time, Ford made sure Nixon received the blessings of liberty just like they wrote it in the Constitution.

This was the world my siblings were born in to. A world where they were deliberately kept from seeing how the system was already at war against them. But as they grew, it was inevitable that they would see that the United States Government didn't care about them, so they all knew they had to find another way to make it.

In Milwaukee, mayors John L. Bohn (1942-1948), Frank P. Zeidler (1948-1960), and Henry W. Maier (1960-1988) held office during this same period. Bohn was born just four years after slavery ended, so he or his family most likely directly benefited from slavery somehow. Some say Zeidler was supportive of civil rights, but he also may have been threatened into not running for office again because for some reason he stepped down. Maier, who served during the 1967 Milwaukee Riots, called in the National Guard when Black residents revolted against racial injustice and police brutality. Yet the City of Milwaukee named a 75-acre festival park after him.

The 1967 Milwaukee Riots began on July 30th because the Black community was tired—tired of the inequalities, tired of being harassed, ignored, and brutalized. National Guards were brought in on August 3rd to "restore order," but no one sheds light on all the injustices against our people which caused the disorder in the first place. 1,740 arrests, and at least 100 civilians injured by Milwaukee Police Department, and the National Guards. White racists, and the Government are always willing to crash out, all because our people want freedom, justice, and equality. If there is anytime having a so called "victim mentality" is ok, it's during these times when we must fight armed police and the armed forces, and we are expected to fight unarmed. They are the cowards though. They won't step foot in the black community without having all the advantages on their side. My family lived through all of this. My brothers and sister were just kids during this time.

Because of Slavery, Jim Crow, and several decades of oppression and injustice against blacks, my family and millions of others like ours were set so far back. We are all just working hard just to get back to 0 by any means.

My family didn't talk much about the Milwaukee riots, or the system. They didn't complain, at least not out loud. They just kept grinding and finding ways to survive.

I've always felt like I had three older brothers and one older sister. My brother DB is actually my first cousin, but in every way that matters, he's my big brother. Maybe losing our mothers—his Aunt Martha and my Aunt Ruby—brought us closer. Losing my mom is something I'll never recover from, but I strive to do my best every day.

DB checks in on me regularly. We talk all the time, and it's never about money. He still pays for my lunch whenever we hang out—nothing says "big brother" more than that. In the winter, when my car is snowed in, DB shows up with his big truck and plow, making sure I'm good like a real big bro. That's just who he is.

He's been hustling since he was 14 years old and never stopped. DB always knew this government didn't care about us, so he figured out his own way too. He's self-taught in everything—DJing, bartending, catering, snow removal, even hosting card games at his house, just like our moms used to do. A real hustler to the core.

Then there's Stan, Ty, and Kat. Stan is one of the funniest people I know. He could have easily been a comedian. Back in Highland, he was the best "ribber" around—nobody could out rank him. I was on the wrong end of his jokes many times as a kid. And his laugh? Easily one of the most disrespectful laughs ever. If he's laughing with you, it's hilarious. But if he's laughing at you, you feel ten times worse. Still, Stan gave me something I'll always be grateful for—he introduced me to hip-hop. From Run-DMC and Biz Markie to Big Daddy Kane and Too Short, I heard it all first from Stan.

Ty, is the smoothest dude I've ever known. If every man carried himself like Ty, the world would be a better place. I always wanted to be like him. I never once heard anybody say Ty did something grimy. He's been through a lot, but he always keeps his cool. On top of that, Ty is a sharp businessman. He and my cousin Chuck were the first Black men I personally knew who owned a business. Back in the late'80s, they opened a restaurant called The Chuckwagon, named after Chuck and the tricked-out station wagon Ty drove back then.

The restaurant was successful, but after my cousin was killed in a robbery in'89, they let it go. Chuck was really ahead of his time. Back when we were growing up in the projects, he bought my Aunt Jo a house on 52nd and Locust. That was unheard of back then. We were on welfare. Not too many people around us was thinking about property ownership, but Chuck was. My Aunt Jo gave birth to Rich, Dale, Chuck, Charlene, San, Kim, Kev Sr., Ken, Plaz Sr., and Claude the Dawg. My Aunt Hyrticina gave birth to Steph, Bren, and Jim Bone. We grew up really close in the projects, but the system was still able to get its grips on some of my relatives. Aunt Hyrticina was the voice of reason. Aunt Ruby? She told you straight up, no filter, and would put you in your place if you got on her bad side. Aunt Jo was the diva, she was always jewelried up. My mom was the cool one.

My sister Kat has always been a presence in my life. She is just like our mom in a lot of my ways. Knows how to cook, keep a clean house, and loves her kids and grandkids. She's also a lot like Aunt Jo. She keeps her hair done, dresses nice, and wears nice jewelry. I see a lot of my aunt ruby's ways in her too, because she loves music and knows how to party. No matter where she lives, she makes it a home. I know she got that from our mom because even in the projects, we had one of the nicest apartments. I know my sister Kat would be an awesome interior decorator if she wanted to. She is also a great mom to her two daughters: Toya and Domo. Kat is an excellent grandma to her grandkids just like my mom and my Aunts Hyrticina, Josie, and Ruby.

My loved ones taught me that the street life is a trap—too much time in the streets and you'd either get locked up or killed. It is better off to just stick with your family and your relatives. My family always stayed close. They would argue, and stop talking to each other, and before you know it, they are all right back together kicking it.

The 4 pillars of hip hop are peace, love, unity, and having fun. I never seen my brother Ty angry, so I always associated him with Peace. I associate my mom with love, because she was the most loving person I ever known. I associate my mom, my sister, Toni, and all my aunts with unity because they always look to keep the family together. Soul food Sundays for us was a prime example of collaborative care. My mom was the best cook I ever known. Anything she cooked seemed like soul food to me. If anyone was hungry, my mom would offer them a plate. Her generosity extended beyond her own children. She would talk with anyone and give them words of encouragement if they would listen.

One of my mom's closest friends was gay, and this was during a time when gay males were treated and talked about very badly in public, but my mom truly loved everybody. She proved that she was all about unity. When I would date white girls, or Latina girls and bring them to our place in the projects she would welcome them with open arms. She would tell me which girls she approved of or didn't approve of based on the girl's character and not the color of her skin. When she told me who she liked the most I kept her around.

DB, Ty, Kat, Stan, and even more recently Ms. Toni are very important to me. My siblings held it down, because I know how hard they worked to make it. My kids and grandkids are my motivation now. I don't know if they will be interested in Music as much as me, but I want them to find whatever they are passionate about and stick with it. I want them to know that having good hobbies will keep them out of trouble, and away from the wrong people. **Stick with family, even when they make you mad sometimes.** I want them to know the United States Government does not care about them, and they will have to find their own way to make it. More than likely, they will have to find jobs, and have good side hustles to live comfortably. Relying on people in the streets or relying on the government is not a good option.

My mom gave me everything I needed to stay off the streets. I introduce positive hip hop to my kids and grandkids. We all know the words to songs like: You Must Learn by KRS-ONE, and Grand Verbalizer by XClan. I always try to have fun with my family and tell them to find their own hobbies. Fall in love with family. As a single dad I do all I can to make sure my kids know I love them and let them know how important it is to keep our unity intact. Listen grandkids, you might as well stay in school and find whatever it is you want to do and master it. Get paid for doing something you like that you can be proud of. Find a hobby that you like. If you can't find a hobby that you like, then support whatever hobby your siblings like. Just don't get caught up in the streets. If you go towards the street life just know there will be conflict. There will be conflict with your siblings too, but that can be resolved. Most people in the streets are already going through so much, they don't know how to resolve conflict. Hurt people will hurt people. 95% of staying out of the system is about knowing how to avoid or resolve conflict in the streets BEFORE police get involved. Some only know how to resolve conflict using their fists, knives, pistols, weapons, or ganging up on people and jumping them. Those are the 85% who I mentioned in the intro. They are pawns in the system, and they fall for every trap easily. On the other hand, real players resolve conflict using the mind. In the game of life, real players don't make the typical moves in the streets and are not so predictable. For example, even though I grew up in the projects with a lot of people, I was always ok being by myself doing what I liked to do. I didn't have to be around everybody all the time. The more people you are around the more likely you will have conflict with some of them. Especially if you are smart, talented, good looking and have money. There will be some haters around you who will be jealous and just not like you.

Being around people who don't like you is not the way to go. They will never like you no matter how nice you try to be to them or how cool you are. They are haters, and the only thing you can do is remove yourself from the situation. You are better off alone than being caught up in the system. Stick with your family. When you have conflict with family it's easier to resolve. The right friends and acquaintances will eventually show up in your life too. They will love you like family. They are like the 5%. They will bring light to your life, and they would never try to hurt you.

God, family, and school is the way to go.

I want young people to ask themselves: Who are the people in your life who check on you when you have nothing to offer? Who supports you without expecting anything in return? Those are your real brothers and sisters—your true family. Family isn't always biological; or bloodline, it's about consistency.

The problems you deal with in the schools you attend now is a small version of what the real-life problems you might experience when you get older. If you hang with the wrong crowd, they'll test your emotions to see if you are weak or strong minded. Your peers will test you to see if they can control you. Picture this: a fight breaks out at school. Who's usually the instigator—the one stirring things up, but just watching when it happens? Who's actually fighting? Who's recording on their phone? Who walks away because they don't want to be involved? Who steps in to break it up?

When the principal asks about it later, you'll see which of your classmates are really the truth. You will realize that a lot of your classmates talk too much. You will notice how they will lie to save themselves, or their reputation. Some will tell the principal whatever they think will get them out of trouble. Then they'll lie to their peers and say they didn't say anything. If they don't tell the principal, they'll tell someone else, and soon the whole school knows. And if you're connected to the situation in any way, you might end up taking the blame. Fingers will point everywhere, reputations will get ruined, and you can't outsmart the principal. The school will protect who they want, and the rest risk expulsion.

That same pattern shows up on the streets when you get older—but the consequences are much heavier. Instead of suspension or expulsion, it could cost you your freedom, your safety, your well-being, or even your life. No matter how good of a person you are, you really can't trust anybody. You must look out for yourself. If you spend too much time with the wrong people, it will eventually cost you.

The streets and the system are tied together. They're designed to pull you out of character, to trap you, to lock you up, or worse. If people are not snitching to police, they are gossiping about each other, to each other. Our communities stay divided. That's why you need smart, positive brothers and sisters around you—people who keep you grounded, uplift you, and help you stay out of trouble.

Chapter 5

My Hood

My Hood Highland Park/Apollo Village 80's

Highland Park Projects is where I got my street sense from. I grew up seeing brothers and sisters doing whatever it took to get their money up, despite knowing the system was against them.

When I mention "the system," you know what it is.

If the system didn't want guns and drugs in the black community, there would be none. If the system wanted to stop the murders, robberies and car thefts in Milwaukee, they could stop it easily. In my opinion, they don't stop it, because the system thrives off black on black violence.

Most of what I'm writing about in this chapter happened between my 10th and 17th birthday. There's no reason for me to talk about the grimy things I saw in the hood, because I never did nothing grimy to nobody. I never set people up to get robbed, never snitched on nobody, and every fight I had was a fair one.

Highland sat in the heart of Milwaukee, Wisconsin. The first time I saw a lot of things was in Highland. That was the first place I stood next to a Cadillac, Porsche, Benz, IROC-Z, Duce N the Quarter, Chevy Caprice Wagon, Corvette, Bonneville, or a Cherokee. Each one of those cars carry a different story. By my 12th birthday, I had already seen or rode in some of the slickest cars anybody could want.

To us, Highland was more than just the projects—it was family. Highland was small enough to where everybody knew each other, but big enough that other neighborhoods in the city didn't try us. I feel fortunate to have come from Highland. I was always close enough to the action to learn the code of the streets directly from the hustlers and thugs in the projects, but I was smart enough to not get involved before I was ready. The most valuable lesson I learned in HP was this: the game is not cool.

From about age 13 on, I was surrounded by some of the richest, coolest street guys you could ever meet. It was a blessing to learn from these guys who had clout and were really living that life. But no matter what, Highland Park Housing Authority ran the projects.

HPHA were part of the system. If the police wanted to raid someone's spot, the Housing Authority was going to let it happen. The hustlers and dealers around me carried themselves with so much good character, style, and class. They weren't like the low-life criminals who ended up on the news every night for doing something silly. If my OG's ended up on the news it would have been for getting money.

I remember the first time I saw a real Rolex—it was on the wrist of a big- time hustler I knew. I asked if he planned to put diamonds on it. He said, "Naw lil bro, when you get you one of these one day, you don't need to put diamonds on it. Don't mess up something that's already a classic." That piece of game stuck with me, and I still use that philosophy in different ways today. By the time I was 14, I already thought like a drug dealer. I remember the first time I saw a kilo of cocaine up close—I thought it was beautiful. In my mind, it looked so pretty you couldn't't do nothing with it but sell it. I saw the smiles those bricks put on the OGs 'faces—They didn't even smile like that at their wives or girlfriends. Those smiles meant they was getting money. By fifteen, I had been put up on so much game that I expected to be fronted at least a" four and a split". Looking back, I'm glad that never happened.

In 1989, I lost a loved one, and that's when I realized the game doesn't love anybody. It's traumatizing to hear a family making funeral arrangements for someone under 25 years old because they lost their life to the streets. It was painful to discover that the people closest to me would cross anybody, rob anybody—or even try to kill anybody—over money or cocaine.

It was tough to see my loved one's have girlfriends or wives who turn out to be gold diggers. From hearing about people I knew overdosing, to me sleeping in "trap" houses, not knowing when it might be raided by the police, or robbed by jealous haters was tough.

Or, how bogus I thought it was when I found out one of my relatives been selling packs to another one of my relatives to get high. Or hearing loved ones talking about getting a lawyer for a friend or associate who caught a drug case— hoping that their friend will appreciate the help and won't turn around and snitch on them.

I could go on and on about things I lived through, but I never complained. I just learned. The ignorant mind will tell a teen something like this: jail, death, snitching, betrayal, and beef are all part of the game. And the younger you are, the easier it is to believe that. But that is not all the way true. The people who loved me made sure I knew the truth: the money, cars, and women might look good, but the game itself is not cool. The D-boy life was never presented to me as sweet—it was presented as business. A dangerous business. In the early mornings when the nice cars were parked and the money was put away in the safe, and my loved ones would be home for a few hours, they would talk about all the reasons they need to get out the game, and why I shouldn't't get in it. They told me I wasn't ready to go all in. They knew all the traps and didn't want me involved. For a while, I listened. Until I didn't.

Highland wasn't just where I learned about the streets; I played a lot of fun games in Highland too. The Highland Park Community Center was our spot. They renamed it the Boys & Girls Club, but we simply called it, "The Buildin". Inside the buildin', we played Ping-Pong, and full court basketball. Outside The Buildin we would go to McDowell playground to play basketball. Outside we would shoot dice too. Sometimes I played the dice games, but some outside games, I knew better than to play. Like the game where dudes ran around the projects with real guns playing "I Could Have Got You." Running up on each other, pulling out pistols, click-clack— "Haha, I could have got you." The lesson? Stay ready, I guess.

Then there was Ninja-Ninja Killer. We loved Karate movies, and watching black belt theatre in the'80s. This game was rough: younger dudes were ninjas, and older dudes were ninja killers. At night they ran all through the projects. If the ninja killers caught a ninja, they'd beat him like they didn't know him. I never played because, as a chubby kid who couldn't't run fast, I would have just slowed the rest of the ninjas down. I went home and played the games I was good at. My Ninja homies would come by my place and tell me about the vicious battles the next day.

I listened to my loved ones. But I must admit, by the time I turn 16 yrs old I started thinking, I needed to get in the game and make me some money, with or without their graces.

Around my sophomore or junior year in Highschool, I linked up with this Vice Lord brother—I'll call him Bruh for book purposes—he was the older brother of a guy I used to hang around with from another block, not too far from Highland. (Bruh was not my real brother). Me and his younger brother would listen to rap music, kick our own lil free styles, and hook up with girls. Bruh heard me rap, and he said he liked it. The more I got to know Bruh our conversations went deeper. I found out that Bruh was from Chicago, and he went back and forth between there and Milwaukee hustling. One day, during one of our conversations, I mentioned my cousin Popsy's name. Popsy was also a Vice Lord from Chicago. Bruh claimed he knew Popsy. I really didn't believe him. He offered to prove it, but I wasn't interested—I didn't want my loved ones to find out and question me about Bruh. So, I just acted like I believed him.

Bruh was an active Vice Lord. Everything in his place was red—leather couches, blinds, rugs, even his cars. My loved ones used to tell me real hustlers stayed out of gang business, but not Bruh. He was in that life, making money, and I was glad he wanted me to be down with him.

I wasn't impressed with the material stuff he had. I grew up seeing hustlers having nice things in the projects. What surprised me was how talented Bruh was. Dude could really sing. He sang like the lead guy of the R&B group Mint Condition. His girl was bad, and she could sing too. When I would go over to his house on 25th street, Bruh and his girl would be singing together. I thought it was funny, but they would be jamming. He could have done major things if he had taken his singing talent seriously, but he chose the streets instead.

Bruh put me up on game, straight up. No sugarcoating nothing. My loved ones cautioned me about the game, but Bruh laid it all out. I was just a teen, but in my mind, I was ready to get this money. I was starting to get serious about rapping, and I was happy to be able to rap about things I really experienced. I was making my own money with Bruh, and nobody could tell me nothing.

Bruh would always say, "We take care of our own." For the most part, he kept his word,...until he didn't. One day at his house, he tried to get me and my homie to smoke a primo. A primo, for those who don't know is weed laced with cocaine. As soon as he lit the weed, I knew it was laced. I already knew what a primo smelled like. I tapped my homie's arm to warn him, but he didn't get it. After my homie smoked it, he said he felt funny, and I saw Bruh kind of smirk about it. It was not funny to me. I didn't smoke it, but my homie and Bruh did. Shortly after, Bruh got up and walked away to go talk to his girl in the other room, I leaned in and told my guy, "Don't hit that weed no more. It's laced." What surprised me was, it didn't seem like my homie cared. Yet and still, so much could have gone down over that. I was glad my homie didn't think I was trying to set him up. He let it go, but I didn't. I decided to distance myself from Bruh after that for good. If I would have hit that primo, it would have been some drama behind that, because I would have told my loved ones. He should have let me and my homie know before he lit the joint what was in it. By the time I turned seventeen, Bruh was locked up. Days turned into years, numbers changed, and we lost contact. I didn't hit that laced joint because my loved ones taught me early—Never smoke something somebody give me because I don't know what they might have put in it.

Was Bruh part of the network of institutions the U.S. government put in place to control neighborhoods in Milwaukee? Could he have been one of the snitches or confidential informants in the neighborhood who cooperate with law enforcement daily? I will never know, because I haven't seen or heard from him or his brother since.

I do know this: The City of Milwaukee, along with its state and local systems and policies, are designed to keep Black people trapped in cycles of poverty, incarceration, or death. My uncle in Chicago used to tell me, "Be careful outside, nephew. If they can't get you in the wash, they'll get you in the rinse." The older I get, the more I understand what he meant. The streets is the wash, and the police is the rinse. If the streets don't get you then the police will because the streets, and the police, are working together. If you get caught up in either one the system wins.

The system is using street dudes as pawns in their larger system of control. Most of the guys you think are bosses in these streets are really just workers. They work for the system, whether they know it or not. When they go to prison and start snitching, their families begin denying it—making excuses or blaming everybody else. That's when the jealousy and envy start to show. Friends and family begin to gossip, and it doesn't matter if what they say is the truth or lies—they're still going to keep talking. Who wants to deal with that constantly? Not me. Now I can tell the youth like my loved ones told me as a kid, leave the streets alone. Surround yourself with people who know how to boss up in different ways. Go to church. I'd rather be in church possibly getting lied to by the preacher man than be in the streets getting lied to—or lied on— by these haters. The preacher might want your money, but at least he'll give you a good scripture to take with you. People in the streets only want what's yours. And if they can't have it, they'll lie on you or try to hurt you some kind of way. In the end, you get nothing in return.

Chapter 6

My City

Might be the only spot where Milwaukeean's have unity.

For years, Milwaukee, Wisconsin, has held the title of the most segregated city in the United States. There's only one place where segregation seems to disappear—when people from all backgrounds head to "Da' Pot" to gamble at the casino. Outside of that, the city remains divided. Milwaukee's Black population sits at around 220,000, nearly equal to the city's white population. You'd think that a city with such a close demographic balance would focus on unity, ensuring fair treatment for all. But instead, at the time of this writing, Milwaukee has the largest racial achievement gap in the nation. 33.4% of black people in Milwaukee live in poverty compared to 7.1% of white households who live in poverty. A Black person in Milwaukee is **twelve times** more likely to be arrested than a white person. Why is it that schools in white neighborhoods receive better funding, or grocery stores are more plentiful in predominantly white areas? How come the best jobs go to white candidates first, while Black workers are left with the scraps? Why are homes in predominantly white communities given more value than homes in predominantly black communities? The reason for these inequalities...MONEY.

For the system to give so much to white people, it must first take from Black people. Redlining, segregation, discrimination, mass incarceration, and police brutality are just some of the tools used to maintain this imbalance. But the most damaging trap the system set was turning Black people against one another.

Many of us grew up in environments where survival meant doing whatever it took to get back what the system took from us—and strategically, it is set up so, the only people within reach for us to take from is our own kind. None of this is accidental—it's all by design. At its core, it's about money and control. When white people control the flow of money, they weaponize it as much as they can to manipulate and suppress poor Black communities. And they can hide behind the system while doing it the entire time.

This is how our people are systematically pushed into survival mode—pimping, robbing, stealing from one another, and even killing—doing exactly what the system wants done. These behaviors are not typical; they're the direct result of what happens when the system takes everything of value from us until there is nothing left but poverty and desperation. And when desperation settles in, it causes many of our brothers and sisters in our neighborhoods to move dangerously.

You better not get caught lacking around somebody who's desperate—because if hurting someone from their own community is the only way they see to get what they want, they will do it. And then there are those who are not out to physically harm nobody, but they'll play mind games—all day, every day—to manipulate or finesse their way to get what they want. That's probably why they call it "the game." And if you are not already aware of what's going on, then somebody in the hood will think it's safe to play games with you.

The survival mindset of many black people—born from poverty and scarcity—is exactly what the system exploits. It doesn't just put us against each other; it recruits from among us too.

The system flips people from our own neighborhoods. It selects certain individuals—usually the ones moving the most dope or pulling the boldest moves—and gives them immunity in exchange for information about other people in the streets. That's how the ones who we thought was the most solid end up as confidential informants. The system knows exactly who the streets admire and/or fear. They target those individuals specifically and turn them into confidential informants.

These informants are likely given a pass to act a donkey in the streets for their cooperation. They can't turn the system down for their own selfish reasons. Little do they know, when the system don't need them no more, they will get tossed out for the next person. If someone you know gets locked up, go read the paperwork on the case, you might find out that someone you thought was solid was working with "them people" the whole time.

There's probably an informant in every neighborhood, gang, crew, and sometimes even in our own families. Undercover agents and confidential informants are all over Milwaukee. And the truth is, it's often someone you know. Someone you respected. Someone you thought was "a real one", is being used as a tool for "them people" behind closed doors. And in the end, that's what's most disappointing. Only thing worse than an informant or snitch is a pedophile.

Even when I see young people out here driving reckless, running red lights, swerving through traffic, I don't even honk my horn at them. I let them go—because I honestly believe some of them gotta be working with police too. No real street dudes would ever drive foolish like that. Most people in the streets with good sense don't want to bring attention to themselves. But some of these dudes probably get a pass to drive reckless in the streets because they are confidential informants. They're out here pretending to be reckless just to set a dangerous trend for everybody else to follow. Then when the rest of us—non informants—try to do the same thing, we will be the ones getting pulled over, ticketed, and/or locked up.

That's the trap, and that's the city for you pretty much. You have those who fake it like they made it but really don't have nothing. Then there are those who made it by working, or got some kind of inheritance, or settlement, but for some reason still want to fake it like they made it from the dope game or off the pistol. Thats how a lot of people on the streets in Milwaukee are moving. But if you being fake on any level at some point you might draw the wrong type of attention to yourself, and the streets will make you pay.

The system knows our neighborhoods can be full of wannabes and copycats. If one person does something, the next person wants to do it too. But what most don't realize is that the one doing it first is likely an informant and protected by the system, while everyone else is walking right into their traps and getting caught up or killed. This is just another tactic the system uses to keep us distracted, divided and trapped. They know how to create an environment of jealousy and envy in the hood to keep people beefing. Be careful in the streets.

Let's examine this in a more playerish perspective. (Part 2)

According to historical records, Milwaukee was founded on January 31, 1846. If we take that claim at face value, it is also important to note that those same records acknowledge that Black people were present in Milwaukee at that time as well. This was during the presidency of James K. Polk, a man who led the country when slavery was still legal, and he had no intention of ending it. Instead of dismantling oppressive structures, he reinforced them—laying groundwork for policies that would allow slavery to keep going strong long after his presidency. Solomon Juneau was elected as the first Mayor of Milwaukee on January 31st 1846. He probably owned slaves or had servants too. The plans for giving white people the unfair advantages, and privileges they have today were being drawn up in 1787. The systems of oppression that uphold white supremacy today were established by the government before Milwaukee became a city in 1846. And the problem is, those systems were never dismantled. They were only refined to keep us down bad. With people like Polk, and Juneau historically in leadership roles it's no wonder why there are minimal opportunities for black people in this city today. They drain our communities for everything we have then shame us when crime and violence go up in this city.

It should be shame on them for needing to design these oppressive systems against us to keep us down. Now more than ever we need to get unified and fight the real enemy so we can dismantle these oppressive systems against us. Real freedom, justice, and equality cannot exist as long as these old, racist structures of this country remain intact. When I mention "the system," I'm referring to the collective of institutions the U.S. government put in place to control people in this country—the police, the military, the legal system, media, religion, financial institutions, and intelligence agencies. Not just the C.I.A or F.B.I, this also includes the snitches and confidential informants on the streets who cooperate with law enforcement daily.

These institutions were designed as a control mechanism to benefit most white people while being weaponized against most Black people in every state. Where is my proof? Let me name off those in Milwaukee who hold leadership roles today: Mayor, Governor, Council men & women, Judges, Fire Chief, County Executive, Aldermen and Alderwomen, Prosecutors, Attorney General, District Attorney, Sheriffs, Police Captain, Senators, wanna be influencers, and hand-picked so called local celebrities around the city. They all work for "the system". They all have some involvement with the collective of institutions the U.S. government put in place to control people in this country(mainly black people.) They all work for or support Trump's MAGA outfit too. None of these so-called leaders in the city did anything about project 2025, and they folded first to end the government shut down. None of them ever openly discuss the need to dismantle the oppressive structures that still impact black people since the constitution was drafted. When was the last time you heard any of these so-called leaders talk about reparations? Under Trump's presidency it's only going to get worse. All these so-called leaders in charge of overseeing the city, yet 33.4% of black residents in Milwaukee still live in poverty. That should be enough proof.

(If not, go ask A.I who are the top 5 racist people in the history of America. When I asked A.I it said 1. President Andrew Johnson, 2. Governor and U.S Senator Theodore Bilbo, 3. Commissioner of Public Safety Eugene "Bull" Connor, 4. Alabama Governor George Wallace, and 5. President Donald Trump.)

It's no coincidence that unregistered guns, weed, cocaine, crack, heroin, fentanyl and all types of other pills continue to flood Black communities. These guns and drugs didn't just appear—they were allowed in for specific reasons. It is reported that the government knows about it, and in certain situations chose to discourage investigations. Drugs and violence exist in white neighborhoods too, but the difference is how the system responds. The system will ensure that Black people are the ones most likely to be murdered or imprisoned because of it, while white people receive protection.

White supremacy isn't about true superiority—it's about control. If white people were naturally supreme, they wouldn't need constant systemic advantages and protection. They wouldn't rely on government policies, media manipulation, economic suppression, or discriminatory policing. They wouldn't need to tempt people in poor communities to pursue the fast life, setting up traps that lead to incarceration or violence. They wouldn't lash out every time black people make progress. True supremacy would be self-evident and fully confident in self—it wouldn't ask for other people to be mistreated if the color of their skin is different.

Yet, many white people cling to figures like Donald Trump because they see him as a safeguard for their privilege. They should know their dominance isn't natural; it's government-backed. If they were truly superior, they wouldn't need unfair advantages to get these big-time careers and high salaries. Michelle Obama said it best: *"We (Black people) will never be afforded the privilege of failing forward."* White privilege allows white people to make mistakes and recover, while Black people are often condemned for life over one misstep.

For me, simply making it through life as a product of my environment without catching a case is something I will always celebrate. I want to show that being a Black man with no criminal record doesn't mean that man never did anything in these streets—it means having the wisdom to recognize the traps and avoid them. Shout out to all the black men and women in Milwaukee who never caught any cases or charges. You never have to snitch if you never get caught up in the system in the first place.

The System Never Forgets, So Why Should We?

Black people are always told to forget the past. Meanwhile, the system itself is designed to never forget anything,....unless it is something that makes white people look bad. Turn on the news, and you'll hear about Milwaukee's crazy weather records dating back to the 1800s. But they will never go that far back to talk about the historical mistreatment of Black people. Why not? Because history exposes the truth. They can't justify the mistreatment of black people so they would rather we all just forget it, and never talk about it. Nobody ever tells Jewish people to forget the holocaust. Every September 11th, we're told to **never forget** What happened in NYC, DC, and PA. Every Fourth of July, we're expected to celebrate white people's freedom from Great Britian. I see Black people proudly wearing red, white, and blue, fireworks filling the sky. But when Juneteenth rolls around the energy is not the same, and no one wants to talk about the race riots that jumped off in Milwaukee on July 30th 1967. Nobody wants to have a conversation about what happened with Lake Ivanhoe which was Wisconsin's first and only black-founded town.

Milwaukee is known as the "city of festivals," but when Black culture is celebrated, it suddenly becomes an issue. In the 1990s, Afro Fest was just as lit—if not more—than Summerfest. But over time, Black celebrations have been diminished, overlooked, or disregarded entirely. I didn't start this division—I was one of those people who believed in supporting everyone. I must admit that changed when I realized the people I supported didn't support the things that mattered to me. Support can't be one-sided if we're supposed to be the "United" States of America.

Milwaukee is cold in the winter, but the weaponization of Segregation is even colder.

Redlining wasn't some random act of discrimination—it was a deliberate strategy created by the government and the banks to keep Black communities, like ours in Milwaukee, trapped in a cycle of poverty while ensuring white communities flourished. Growing up in Highland Projects, I never thought about why we were poor. The projects were fun to me…until it wasn't. Why were we so desperate to get our families out of the projects? The lure of getting money and getting out of the projects made my loved ones desperate to get money and accept whatever risks that comes with it. That desperation led to some bad decisions, and those bad decisions led some of them straight to prison.

Where a person chooses to live may be a personal decision, but systemic oppression isn't. When a white person buys a home for his/her family, they probably never question the high appraisals they receive for their purchase, accepting it as legitimate. It's possible that systemic oppression against Black people goes over the heads of millions of white people—not because it isn't real, but because they've never had to see it. Many remain unaware of how their elders and ancestors carefully designed these systems to work in their favor, all while whitewashing the mistreatment of Black communities in the process.

Most of the white people I know probably grew up believing that their parents succeeded purely through hard work. They probably were raised up believing that their parents and grandparents were honest, fair, salt-of-the-earth people. What they likely weren't taught is that their great-great-great-grandparents probably built their family's foundation off slavery—and that they still benefit from it today, whether they acknowledge it or not.

This is probably why so many white fathers don't want their daughters dating Black men—especially those who are unapologetically black. A "real one" wouldn't shy away from telling the white man's daughter the truth about her family's history. A "real one" would say the same things to her father's face—not out of anger, but out of honesty. And if they were really good people they would accept the truth from the black man and fight for change.

Conversations about systemic privilege often leave out how slavery and oppression gave white families a massive head start—one that continues to this day. When they act like they don't benefit from or even acknowledge the achievement gaps likely caused by centuries of slavery and oppression, it must be poor mental health leaving them in denial. When they act like they are unaware that the same banks that will approve their loans at favorable rates have historically denied loans to Black communities it's just lies and delusion. But ignorance isn't an excuse. Even a 12-year-old can recognize how government policies and racist institutions work together to ensure that everything works in white people's favor. Their advantages were never about being smarter or more capable—just more privileged.

For decades, Black families in Milwaukee were denied bank loans to purchase or renovate homes. Lenders labeled our neighborhoods as "hazardous" and "unworthy of investment." The government and banks who orchestrated this system colluded with these lenders. They drew red lines around Black communities on maps and declaring, "No loans here." This wasn't about property values—it was about their evil agenda against black people.

Meanwhile, those same lenders will grant loans to less qualified white people with no problem. White neighborhoods receive better funding, nicer parks, and more businesses. Still, when I look at houses on Milwaukee's Northside, I don't see any major differences between them and houses in West Allis or Wauwatosa. In fact, I'd argue some Milwaukee homes are nicer than what you'll find in West Allis, and Tosa. However, the property values tell a different story—stories controlled by discriminatory financial institutions. Institutions who can just raise and lower property values anytime they want.

Personally, I love Milwaukee's Northside. Could I move elsewhere? Sure. I've had apartments in Wauwatosa, spent time in Oak Creek, and I could afford a place in Brookfield if I wanted to live there. But why would I spend money to live in an area where my family and I would be harassed by racist neighbors? Why would I want to live in a place where people probably would actively go out of their way to make me feel uncomfortable?

Currently I live on a diverse block in Milwaukee county, with Black and white residents alike. But I can't say whether the banks gave my white neighbors a better deal on their homes than I got for mine. That's a conversation most aren't ready to have.

Job Discrimination.

Job discrimination is another one of segregation's most damaging effects. A lack of diversity in the workplace stifles success of the company, yet many companies still refuse to recognize this. Sometimes I think these companies would rather fail than promote a black person into a leadership role that could possibly save them. They allow racial biases to influence hiring and promotions, leading to unqualified white employees being chosen over highly qualified Black candidates. Businesses that operate this way will eventually fail because they ignore the reality that diversity increases chances for success. End of the day they know they can count on the government to bail them out in some way.

Segregation makes whiteness a tool—a weapon—that extends beyond housing and education. White people use employment to exclude us. They use the police as their enforcers. If you don't want to live near me, fine. But don't deny me economic opportunities because of my skin color.

The Truth Shall Always Triumph

The erasure of Black history and the celebrations of black achievements isn't an accident. It's intentional. Haters like Trump and Elon Musk want to rewrite history, roll back progress, and whitewash the truth. But we know what it is. Any Black person with the ability to write a book, make content, or document our history should always speak truth to so called power.

Huey Newton once said: "Anytime the Black man attempts to change the slave image; it scares white people." That fear is real. The government knows that if Black people ever get unified, we would overcome all of the systems built to oppress us. America can never be truly great until **freedom, justice, and equality** are not just words, but realities—for all people. Milwaukee can never be great until black people get the proper recognition, and respect we deserve.

Get Active:

It's one thing to acknowledge systemic inequalities; it's another to dismantle it. Here's how individuals, communities, and organizations who want to fight against systemic inequalities in Milwaukee and beyond can get active.

1. Understanding the System

Knowledge is power. If you don't understand how systemic racism operates, you can't fight it. Start by educating yourself and others. The United States is ran like a company not a country. It has C.E.O's, presidents, vice presidents, managers, and all they care about is money not people. They need a lower class so they can pay cheap or no labor costs to the poor. All while keeping themselves in high rank high paid positions.

- Read books like Message To The Blackman In America by The Honorable Elijah Muhammad and *A Promised Land* by Barack Obama.
- Study Milwaukee's history of redlining (look up maps that show how Black neighborhoods were boxed out of loans and resources).
- Follow local activists, journalists, REAL hip hop artists, poets, politicians and scholars who not only speak on Milwaukee's racial disparities, but will do something.

◆ **Exercise:** Research your neighborhood's history. What policies shaped it? Who benefits from them today?

2. Strengthening Black Economics

Money is power, and systemic racism has always been about economic control.

- Support Black-owned businesses and encourage others to do the same.
- Bank with Black-owned credit unions and push for community reinvestment.
- Invest in land and property within Black neighborhoods to prevent gentrification.
- Look for careers in Law enforcement, look to become Lawyers, Doctors, and Scientist.

◆ **Exercise:** Every month, challenge yourself to spend at least 25% of your money at Black-owned businesses. Document the impact.

3. Holding Institutions Accountable

- Demand transparency from Milwaukee's police department. Advocate for community oversight boards.
- Challenge companies that practice ANY type of discrimination or harrassment in hiring and promotions.
- Push for fair school funding to ensure children who live in our communities receive quality education.
- Send youth to good after school programs that will keep them from off the streets and out the way of temptation where many of the systemic traps are set.

◆ **Exercise:** Contact your city council representative. Ask them what they're doing to address racial disparities in Milwaukee.

4. Political Action and Policy Change

Racism and inequality are issues because the laws allow it. If we want real change, we must challenge these laws.

- Vote in **local elections**—these impact policing, schools, and housing.
- Support policies that promote equity in homeownership, employment, and criminal justice.
- Demand reparations and financial programs that correct past injustices in Milwaukee.

◆ **Exercise:** Organize or support a voter registration drive in your community.

5. Community Empowerment

- Start or support mentorship programs that support youth and young adult professionals.
- Create self-sustaining Black neighborhoods with urban farming, cooperatives, and independent schools.
- Build community safety initiatives that don't rely on the police.
- Just stay out of trouble as much as you can.

◆ **Exercise:** Volunteer for a local nonprofit working to uplift youth and young adults in the 414.

Just Keeping It 100

The systemic division and segregation in Milwaukee isn't just history—it's still happening right now. But history also shows that when Black people want change, we create change. Just like our elders did on July 30th 1967 in the Milwaukee Riots.

With God first all things are possible. Milwaukee has the potential to be a city that works for everyone, not just a select few. But it won't happen if we leave it up to those currently in power to fix it. Faith without work is futile. I'm not trying to send you to church. I'm trying to send you to the streets, to the local businesses, and to the voting booths to create change.

May the divine spirit be with you. It starts with us. It gets handled by us.

Ask yourself:
- What role do I play in either upholding or dismantling these systems?
- How can I use my skills, resources, and voice to make change?
- Am I willing to do the work to create a better Milwaukee for future generations?

This isn't just about race. It's about having true freedom, justice and equality right here in Milwaukee.

The question is—are you about that life?

*

Chapter 7

My Understanding

My understanding is this: This city allows Milwaukee Police Department to do whatever they want with little to no accountability. Prosecutors have the power to pursue charges against whomever they choose, or they can let suspects walk free based on personal discretion. The courts can convict or release people anytime they want. When it comes to the Black community, the laws seem to bend. It all depends on how they feel like interpreting the law in that moment, case by case. If you a real street dude who not working for them people, the system will not work in your favor. Therefore, A Black man never catching a case, and never getting caught up in the system, is a real win for the hood—especially when you consider the odds stacked against us from birth. It's not about staying out of trouble; it's about surviving a system that was never meant for us.

The government has always used systems and tactics to divide, manipulate, and distract people. Black people have never been welcomed—only used. Used as scapegoats when the non elite white people start pressuring the government looking for bailouts after their own failures. Behind closed doors the government probably says to them, "We're doing all we can to stop blacks from taking your place," while quietly plotting on everyone beneath the so called elite.

The middle class and poor white folks should know they're also being lied to. They see the cracks in their own communities. But instead of accepting the truth—that the rich are hoarding power—they go back and forth with their stances over the nonsense myth that Black progress comes at their expense. It's classic deflection.

Even historically, some white families were robbed—tricked out of their land and livelihood by wealthier whites. This is why the articles of the confederation was replaced with the constitution. But instead of seeing common ground with us, they were taught to stay away from Black people, unless it somehow benefited them more.

My understanding is, we're fighting two systems:

One built to keep Black people down by any means necessary. Another built to keep poor and working-class white people frustrated. Whites are allowed to get closer to the top than most black people, but they also see the shadiness at play. **The Government fears an alliance between anti-war, anti-racist white activists, and non-sellout Black people.** If we united together against those who are in control of government, we could really make America great for the first time ever.

The government's main concern isn't justice—it's to secure the Blessings of Liberty for white people. They craft laws with one purpose: to control the masses so their own selfish desires can continue to go on unchecked. So I ask: are laws even real? Or are they simply tools of manipulation and control?

From the beginning, America was built on greed. The laws were written to serve the powerful, not the people. They decided who "deserved" power, not based on merit or morality, but on status and skin color. That's why the system still doesn't work—it will never work under those circumstances.

And so, when a Black man walks through life in America untouched by their machine, it's more than luck—it's a blessing. It's a win.

The Constitution:

A Document formed on Contradiction and Slavery. The United States Constitution is a document that has been praised as the supreme law of the land. It was signed on Sept. 17, 1787 by 39 white dudes, and ratified the next year. Starting as a document composed of a Preamble and seven Articles, it has been amended 27 times. But let's be clear: The Constitution was drawn up by white people for white people. Of the 39 delegates who signed it, all were white men — and at least 23 of them were slave owners or profited directly from the slave trade. They were white men who had actively supported, benefited from, and in many cases violently defended the institution of slavery. Many white people today are direct descendants of these guys and are recipients of what they left behind.

This is the list of white men who signed the Constitution who also owned slaves by state:

Virginia:

1. George Washington – Owned slaves.

2. James Madison – Lifelong slaveholder; called slavery a "difficult question."

3. George Mason –Owned slaves.

4. John Blair – Owned slaves.

5. Edmund Randolph – Owned slaves.

South Carolina:

6. Charles Cotesworth Pinckney – Strong advocate for protecting slavery.

7. John Rutledge – Defended slavery at the convention.

8. Pierce Butler – Major rice plantation owner; vocal supporter of defending slavery.

Georgia:

9. William Few – Owned slaves.

10. Abraham Baldwin – Owned slaves.

North Carolina:

11. William Blount – Owned slaves.

12. Richard Dobbs Spaight – Owned slaves.

13. Hugh Williamson – Likely a slaveowner (not much documentation, but highly probable).

Maryland:

14. Daniel of St. Thomas Jenifer – Owned slaves.

15. James McHenry – Owned slaves.

Delaware:

16. Richard Bassett – Owned slaves.

17. Jacob Broom – Owned slaves.

Pennsylvania:

18. Robert Morris – Profited heavily from the slave trade.

19. Thomas Fitzsimons – Involved in trade, including goods tied to slavery.

New York:

20. Alexander Hamilton – Owned slaves

Connecticut:

21. William Samuel Johnson – Owned slaves.

22. Roger Sherman – Owned slaves.

New Jersey:

23. William Livingston – Owned slaves.

Massachusetts:

(To me, anything with the word Massa in it got slave maker of the poor energy on it)

I'm sure Ms Toni, who graduated from Rufus King High School is glad to know Rufus King did not own slaves. He is reported as someone who spoke against slavery. But he did sign the constitution, so he hung out with dudes who did own slaves. They were his homies.

39 white dudes signed the Constitution. That means 16 delegates did not sign.

Key Reasons Why Delegates Refused to Sign the Constitution:

1. Belief the Constitution gave too much power to the federal government

Several delegates thought the new Constitution created a central government that was too powerful and threatened the rights of states and individuals.

• George Mason (Virginia) – Refused to sign because the Constitution did not include a Bill of Rights.

• Elbridge Gerry (Massachusetts) – Opposed the lack of a Bill of Rights and worried about excessive federal power.

• Edmund Randolph (Virginia) – Helped write the document but didn't sign, saying it needed more safeguards and state consensus.

2. Opposition to slavery

Very few unnamed delegates opposed the protections the Constitution gave to slavery.

• Luther Martin (Maryland) – Strongly opposed slavery and walked out of the Convention.

3. Left the Convention early or didn't attend regularly

Some delegates simply left before the signing due to personal reasons, political frustration, or state duties.

• Alexander Martin (North Carolina) – Left early.

• William Houston (New Jersey) – Illness prevented regular participation.

• George Wythe (Virginia) – Left the Convention early due to personal obligations.

• Robert Yates and John Lansing Jr. (New York) – Left early, believing the Convention should have amended the Articles of Confederation instead of drafting a new Constitution.

4. Believed it lacked democratic protections

A few felt the Constitution wasn't democratic enough and gave too much power to elites.

• Caleb Strong (Massachusetts) – Supported the Constitution but didn't sign due to being called home early.

• James McClurg (Virginia) – Left before the signing; wanted a stronger executive branch but left when his views weren't accepted.

It's a shame that only two named persons opposed slavery when the constitution was being drafted.

Before the Constitution, the United States was governed by a document called the Articles of Confederation. This created a system where the individual states held most of the power, while the federal government role was very minimal. Imagine Wisconsin having complete authority to make its own laws without any interference from the federal government. Each state essentially ruled its own territory and operated independently.

Yet even with all that unchecked authority, the white dudes who wrote the constitution still couldn't get along. They fought over taxes and trade, over land and power. At that time, it was not the federal government role to collect taxes or enforce laws. The United States had trouble paying off debts from the Revolutionary War. They were not trusted by foreign nations to pay back their debts.

There were rebellions going on at the time like the shay's rebellion. The system was buckling because of poor leadership. **They depended on the free labor of our ancestors for survival. Slavery upheld their economy and helped white people pay their debts and make profits. Enslaved people built the infrastructure, grew the crops and earned the profits that enabled the U.S. to endure. Our ancestors worked without receiving credit, compensation or protection under the law.**

White people moved on from the Articles of the confederation to a new system — The Constitution. This was a new model, one that centralized their power but preserved slavery. That's the genesis of the Constitution: not only to make "a more perfect union," but to build wealth, maintain order and, **ensure, through the free labor of Black people, that America would thrive.**

So when we say Black people built this country, it's not a stretch. It's fact.

And though many revere the constitution, it is drenched in the blood of our black ancestors. **Fast forward to today:** anyone who choose to ignore or disregard the violent, slaveholding, foundational era of the Constitution is not defending democracy — they are defending murder. White people are the ones who should have been incarcerated for all the years of slavery, jim crow, and all of the hate crimes against black people that continued to happen for decades afterwards. The incompetence and greed that produced the constitution still affects us today. It is built into a system designed to secure the Blessings of Liberty to white people.

The U.S. Constitution begins with the Preamble:
"We the People of the United States, in Order to form a more perfect Union, establish Justice, ensure domestic

tranquility, provide for the common defense, promote the general Welfare, and **secure the Blessings of Liberty to ourselves and our Posterity**, do ordain and establish this Constitution for the United States of America."

While these words sound noble, the reality is that "We the People" did not include Black people. This so-called "more perfect Union" was created by white men, for white men.

77 years after the constitution slavery was abolished—on January 18, 1865—when the 13th Amendment was ratified. White people had a head start like no other. Most of them are still ok with the fact that hundreds of thousands of black people were violently forced to work for them for free for at least 77 years straight.

The 13th Amendment states:

"Neither slavery nor involuntary servitude, <u>except as a punishment for crime</u> whereof the party shall have been duly convicted, shall exist within the United States, or any place subject to their jurisdiction."

That "except as punishment for a crime" part? That's the loophole that keeps slavery legal through incarceration. If you're convicted of a crime, and sent to prison or jail you are a slave. The state will force you to work for little or no pay— just like a slave. That is why **I'M NOT GOING**, unless it's for something worth it.

June 19th, or Juneteenth, commemorates the day in 1865 when slavery officially ended—but only in name, not in practice. Don't get it confused, our ancestors fought their way out of slavery. White people didn't just grow a good conscious and let our ancestors free, because after slavery Jim Crow era began.

Fast forward to today, and the system is still working against Black people. Prisons are incentivized to stay full. Many private prison companies have contracts with the government that pay them a fixed amount per inmate, per day—regardless of whether the prison is full. So, to "get their money's worth," states push for higher incarceration rates. These profit-driven prisons can use their money and influence to lobby for harsher laws, pressure judges for longer sentences, and push policies that keep people behind bars. The system is designed to keep beds full, and it's no coincidence that Black people are the main targets.

Why Black people? Because that clause in the 13th Amendment opened the door. Slavery was "abolished"—except for those convicted of crimes. So, they made being Black a crime. The stats don't lie: Black people make up about 12% of the U.S. population, yet nearly half the prison population. In Wisconsin, it's even worse. Black people are incarcerated at a rate 11.8 times higher than white people. One in every 36 Black adults in Wisconsin is in prison—the highest rate in the country. We make up just 6% of the state's population but account for 42% of its prison population.

And through all of that? I ain't never caught a case.

When a Black man walks through the streets of any city in America untouched by the system, that's a win for the streets. I never caught a case, so I could never be a snitch. I never worked for the system. My family is from the streets for real. That's why I move how I move. Some may call me old school, but I call it longevity. I don't make it easy for police to have a reason to pull me over or harass me. I keep my license, registration, and insurance up to date. I don't drive reckless. I don't hang out in predominantly white areas of Milwaukee where I know I'm not welcome and could easily be criminalized for anything.

I know what the system is, and I'm careful about how to move through it to avoid becoming another statistic as much as possible.

Craig Brown

*

Chapter 8

The War

Some of the men in my family joined the military. I can only hope that part of their decision to enlist was driven by a desire to fight for civil rights and equality from within the system. The rest of the men in my family lived the street life. To me, it didn't make much of a difference—military or the streets—it was all part of the same system. A system designed to trick them out of becoming representatives of any political or civil rights movement. We often end up fighting in wars abroad for a country that don't value us or fighting each other in the streets over blocks we don't own. But rarely are we encouraged to fight the very system that's been fighting us for generations. MAGA white people will turn a blind eye to anything to keep white privilege intact.

In the 1950s, Dwight D. Eisenhower was president. But behind the scenes, it was J. Edgar Hoover who was calling the shots. He spied on every single Black leader. He launched COINTELPRO in 1956, supposedly to disrupt "left-wing organizations." But all the men in my family ever taught me about was how deep this Government's hatred ran for Black voices. Hoover criminalized the Black Panthers. Hoover went after Malcolm X. He targeted Dr. Martin Luther King Jr. Hoover wasn't just fighting against civil rights—he was fighting for white privilege.

The fight for true freedom, justice, and equality *within* the system is the only fight that should matter to Black people. In my opinion, it's the only fight worth catching a case for.

The war on black people is still going on right now, whether you choose to fight back or not is on you.

The American Revolutionary War took place from 1775 to 1783. During this time, Black people played a huge role in helping white americans gain their freedom from King George III of Great Britain. However, the British saw an opportunity—they began recruiting our ancestors. The British people offered our ancestors weapons to fight against the white americans here in the United States. Thousands of our ancestors joined the British army, choosing to fight against the American slave makers who had kept them in bondage. Many even fled to Great Britain to support the British cause.

George Washington recognized the threat this posed to America's fight for independence. He knew that if all Black people sided with the British, the United States most likely would lose the war. In response, Washington made a promise: if Black people fought for America, they would gain their freedom. Trusting this promise, our ancestors took up arms for the United States—and America won the war.

But after securing victory, America turned its back on our ancestors. Instead of granting freedom, this nation pushed our ancestors even deeper into slavery. Since then, this country has continued to lie to us.

I envision the scenario happening again. I vision somebody major like China offering to put some of their high tech weapons in our hands to help us fight against our oppressors here in America. I vision Black people working with other nations to help us fight for the freedom, justice, and equality we truly deserve. Since the United States current administration is not putting any respect on our name, we should be willing to accept aid from other nations—Canada, China, or any country that recognizes our value. If we moved as a unified nation, we would gain international respect and have the power to make our own deals, just like the people of Ukraine. **There are roughly 40 million Ukrainians in Europe, and there are about 40 million Black people in America. If they can fight for their sovereignty, why shouldn't we?**

The U.S. government continues to build America for the benefit of white people while consistently overlooking Black communities. But on a global scale, other countries know about our black excellence. We can negotiate with Mexico, the

Middle East, Africa—whoever we choose. America wants to keep us in a subordinate position, but we don't have to accept that. I vision a time when our people start thinking and moving as a nation.

Their weapons of choice in this war against us are: Police, AI, education, employment, finance, debt, and social media. I worked at a multi-billion dollar telecommunication company and I can tell you from experience the leadership positions are quickly offered to white people, or people from other ethnicities who are less qualified than many black people. As far as finance goes, one time I got close to an 800 credit score. I maintained that score for several years. I missed one payment that I didn't know was due, and they drop my score down to 556. I made the payment that I missed the same day, but they didn't restore my credit score back to what it was as fast as they dropped it. I never thought about how my rapid credit score drop to unfavorable status systemically blocks me from wealth building opportunities.

Here is how Equifax, Experian, TransUnion, and FICO Reinforce Racial Discrimination

The U.S. credit system, dominated by the three major credit bureaus—Equifax, Experian, and TransUnion and FICO (Fair Isaac Corporation) credit scoring models have long been criticized for perpetuating systemic racism and economic inequality. While the explicit racism may not be evident in the language of the credit reports, it is reflected in the ways the credit bureaus respond to different groups of people. A tool that claims to objectively assess financial reliability, in reality, is inherently biased against Blacks. This makes upward mobility more difficult for us. Historical discrimination, limited access to credit-building opportunities, and entrenched economic disparities make Black Americans prime targets of this system.

Hated Till We Make It.

The racial wealth gap, a legacy of centuries of policies such as slavery, Jim Crow laws, redlining, and exclusion from New Deal housing programs, means that Black families inherit little wealth compared to their white counterparts. And because credit scores are heavily weighted on financial history, a Black person born into poverty is systematically penalized at every turn. According to studies, Black consumers tend to have lower average credit scores than their white counterparts. This disparity, however, is not the result of financial mismanagement; rather, it is rooted in structural barriers to wealth accumulation, such as discrimination in employment, education, and homeownership.

Money In The Ghetto.

FICO and other credit scoring models use factors that disproportionately harm Black people:

Payment History (35% of score):

If my payment history is exemplary, why does TransUnion lower my score so drastically for a single late payment? This seems to be a design to hinder my ability to build wealth. Many Black households, traditionally excluded from mainstream banking, rely on alternative financial services like payday loans, which are not reported to credit bureaus, yet still negatively impact credit scores. Late payments are often the result of economic instability, which disproportionately affects Black communities due to wage disparities and job discrimination.

Credit Utilization (30% of score):

Since Black people generally earn lower wages and salaries at our jobs, it's more likely that we carry higher credit balances relative to our credit limits, which lowers our scores.

Credit History Length (15% of score):

Historically, Black people have been excluded from mainstream banking, leading to shorter credit histories compared to those who have had consistent access to financial services. This makes it harder to build strong credit profiles.

Credit Type (10% of score):

Other consumers are often offered lower-interest loans and rewards for their financial behavior, Black consumers are more likely to turn to high-interest department store cards, payday loans, or check-cashing services, all of which negatively impact credit scores.

Dirty Money
Redlining & Mortgage Discrimination:

Banks that once denied loans to Black people now rely on credit scores that reflect the lower incomes of minority groups, categorizing them as higher-risk borrowers and charging higher interest rates or outright denying them loans. Even with the same credit score, Black borrowers are often denied loans or charged higher interest rates compared to their white counterparts, further limiting their ability to accumulate wealth.

Predatory Lending & Subprime Loans:

During the 2008 financial crisis, Black borrowers were disproportionately targeted for subprime mortgages, even when they qualified for better terms. The resulting foreclosure crisis wiped out an entire generation of Black wealth, while many white borrowers were unaffected.

Racial Disparities in Debt Collections:

Small unpaid debts—such as credit card bills, utility accounts, or student loans—can do harm to our credit ratings.

For example, I was close to an 800 FICO score and missed one student loan payment just once. TransUnion dropped my score to 556 points, with no warning or consideration of my consistent payment history. I got my credit back right anyway, but still.

Psycho FICO.

More than just securing loans, FICO scores influence employment opportunities, housing, car insurance, and utility bills, all of which compound existing economic inequalities. High-income Black individuals still suffer from low credit scores due to the long-lasting effects of discriminatory financial practices. This makes upward mobility difficult, even for those who have overcome economic barriers.

Moreover, credit bureaus make it incredibly difficult to correct errors in their reports. Black consumers, who are more likely to experience identity theft and fraud, bear the brunt of this flawed system.

The need for Credit Reform.

Address racial discrimination in credit scoring, many activists and economists advocate for:

Alternative credit scoring models

that account for rent, utility payments, and other on-time bills, which would disproportionately benefit Black consumers.

Stronger regulations

to prevent discrimination in lending, credit reporting, and debt collection.

Increased accountability

for the banks and credit bureaus that continue to uphold these discriminatory practices.

While Equifax, Experian, TransUnion, and FICO claim to provide "objective" financial assessments, their models were built on a foundation of racial discrimination, systematically excluding Black consumers from wealth-building opportunities. Without significant reform and new regulations, the credit system will continue to perpetuate racial economic disparities.

RICO (Racketeer Influenced and Corrupt Organizations) Law

Originally designed to dismantle organized crime syndicates like the Mafia, RICO is now being used to target Black communities, and famous rappers.

The racism in RICO is not in the text itself, but in how it is enforced, prosecuted, and interpreted.

RICO targets Black communities, criminalizes rappers' lyrics, and perpetuates racial disparities in sentencing.

Selective Enforcement and Over-Policing of Black Communities

RICO is now being used against hip-hop artists and rap groups. Young Thug and YSL are recent examples of this trend, but them laws was trying to lock up Sacramento rapper CBo over his lyrics back in 1998. The so-called "hip-hop police" force, established in 2004, has been tasked with investigating crimes related to hip-hop culture. This selective targeting of Black artists is a continuation of the long-standing criminalization of Black culture.

RICO Trippin

In RICO cases, Black defendants often receive harsher treatment than white defendants charged with similar crimes.

For example, many Black defendants are low-level street guys with little or no connection to the organizations they are charged with associating. Meanwhile, white-collar criminals engaged in high-stakes financial fraud rarely face RICO charges.

Media-Malicious Etiolated Devils Immoral Assignments

The media plays a critical role in shaping public perception of RICO cases. Black defendants are often portrayed as dangerous gang leaders, reinforcing negative stereotypes. In contrast, white defendants are typically depicted as "bad apples," an individualizing standard not given to Black organizations.

Reform Fico & Rico

RICO is part of a broader history of using legal means to suppress and incarcerate Black organizations or individuals. From FBI COINTELPRO targeting the Black Panthers in the 1960s to the War on Drugs, which disproportionately affected African Americans, RICO has been a tool for undermining Black economic and political power. These disparities highlight the urgent need for criminal justice reform, limitations on RICO's sweeping powers, and protection for cultural self-expression, particularly within African American communities.

FICO and RICO are two tools used to prevent Black people from accessing wealth—tools that continue to exploit and reinforce systemic racism in both financial and legal systems. As I have mentioned earlier, poverty leads to desperation, desperation leads to bad decisions, and bad decisions can lead to incarceration. The City of Milwaukee counts on it.

The War Against Black People Never Ended.

White people in positions of power will continue passing down the blueprint for privilege from one white generation to the next. If they can help it, this system of white privilege will not disappear because they value the advantages they have too much. They don't care if the advantages they hold are unfair, and illegitimate. In fact, they become upset when we call out their lies and deceit to get ahead at our expense. White people often react with anger when it is pointed out that they have never had to "pull themselves up by their own bootstraps." For centuries, white people have benefited from handouts and government assistance. They try to use reverse psychology, accusing individuals like me of having a victim mentality. However, the fact remains, white people have had access to the presidency, law enforcement, the judicial system, religion, money, and technology in ways black people never had. Yes, I am a victim of America's systemic hate crimes. As long as it can be proven that white people still benefit from the free labor of my ancestors, then we are not on an even playing field.

The ancestors of white people were murderers, slave owners, and rapists. It was wrong, and they don't want to be reminded of it. They prefer to live in the illusion that their ancestors were good people, but they were not. They want to believe their ancestors were successful because of their own merit, but that is not the case. The first sixteen Presidents were slave owners. They need to be reminded that their success was built on slavery. Their ancestors lied, cheated, and committed murder to establish white privilege, and they continue to live off the wealth and privileges that resulted from it till this day.

True leaders lead by example—through action, positive attitude, and high integrity. Unfortunately, I don't see these qualities in either past or present Presidents of the United States. All I see is greed. What kind of example can I advise my children or grandchildren to follow when considering dudes like Trump or Elon Musk? The only lesson I can give to my grandchildren is that their white peers could grow up and be felons, face sexual assault charges, and still become President of the United States. Meanwhile, I would have to tell my grandchildren that they will need to be nearly perfect, like Barack Obama, to have the same opportunities.

One of my favorite books is Message to the Blackman in America by The Honorable Elijah Muhammad. I often refer to this book to get my mind right. It provides me with a clear vision of what Black people in Milwaukee need to do in order to rise above the traps set by lawmakers who implement systemic policies in this country.

First, we must acquire our own land and property. We need to accept the reality that white people will continue to block the reparations we are owed. With this in mind, we must start finding ways to obtain and maintain land and property.

Second, we must begin and support our own businesses. We need to develop the mindset of exclusively shopping at Black-owned businesses. Whatever you need, check to see if a Black-owned store has it in stock first before you check anywhere else.

Third, we must vote as a collective unit. Ice Cube supported this through the Contract With Black America, which was a step in the right direction.

Lastly, we need to unite to strengthen education and youth and young adult development.

If we do our part to help strengthen black consciousness, and the common sense in youth, and young adults it will help them stay out of jail, prison, and out of an early grave over senseless actions.

Chapter 9

The Conclusion

In the Holy Qur'an, Chapter 83, Al-Tatfif, verses 7-9 state: "Nay, surely the record of the wicked is in prison. And what will make thee know what the prison is? It is a written book."

Maulana Muhammad Ali interprets this as a record of one's actions, where the deeds of wrongdoers are preserved, symbolizing a prison that restrains their ability to do good, ultimately hindering their progress.

When the Holy Qur'an says, "the wicked", I believe it describes whoever is calling the shots for the US government, and the White House. They are the wicked ones. Their record of wickedness and privilege over black people in America is not a display of real power and superiority like they think it is. In reality, they are only creating a spiritual prison for themselves through their wicked deeds. These law makers are constantly creating worldly positions of power for themselves. But ultimately their outcome will be a self-destructive journey towards spiritual confinement. They just can't see past their own greed and wickedness. These devils have a false sense of power. They don't realize how their selfish desires for white privilege and white supremacy have restrained their ability to do good at the spiritual level. The record of their wicked deeds, and wrong doings are preserved in a book with God. That is their prison.

I never caught a case, but they did. They caught a case for historically using their tricks, schemes, and systems to mistreat black people/African Americans. They will have to deal with God--The ultimate judge, and best knower for their constant mistreatment of black people.

From slavery to Jim Crow, from the War on Drugs to mass incarceration, the system has always been dangerous and tricky for Black men and women in America. It is not just about prisons or police—it's about their entire web of institutions built to trap us: the streets, the courts, schools, banks, jobs, housing, media, and politics. They were designed to push us toward desperation so they can punish us when we react. These set up tactics need to be called out.

I was born in December 1976. Gerald Ford was still President of the United States, but Jimmy Carter was set to take office in January 77. United States Government was still openly waging war on Black progress. From 1944 the year my mom was born, to 1976, every U.S. president—from FDR to Ford—upheld policies that favored white people and suppressed black people.

From 1976 to this day, NO PRESIDENT EVER DID ANYTHING FOR BLACK PEOPLE. Jimmy Carter (1977-1981), Ronald Reagan (1981-1989), George H.W. Bush (1989-1993), Bill Clinton (1993-2001), George W. Bush (2001-2009), Barack Obama (2009-2017), Trump (2017-2021), Biden (2021-2025), and now Trump again. And Trump's whole agenda is to roll back any amount of progress black people have made in history at all.

But, even with the deck stacked against us, some of us still learned the game. We didn't fall for the traps. Staying free wasn't fear or luck—it was discipline, awareness, and pure grace. Knowing when to walk away, how to move strategically, and how to protect yourself is what it's all about.

We live in a country that don't care if Black men and women fail. Their concern for Black Americans extends only as far as it benefits white people agendas. They profit when our people get locked away. They love it when they turn the guys and girls from our blocks that we thought were solid into snitches and rats. They think their prison systems should be a display of how powerful they are. But they are upset because no matter how elaborate they think their traps are, they are still a small thing to God. Every law written to suppress us, every policy passed to exclude us, every act of greed or violence against our people—those records are kept with God.

So, when a Black man or woman makes it through life without ever catching a case, it's a blessing. It is also a middle finger up from us to the wicked design of this system. It is proof that God is more powerful than their systems.

I was raised by the most street savvy people, but I had to learn how to survive these traps on my own. My loved ones couldn't teach me everything. I didn't want to have to run to family or friends for protection every time these devils or somebody in the streets tried me. Standing on my own was the only way. I saw the consequences up close. I saw what happens when someone gets fronted some work and try to run off with the money—or lie and say the money or work got stolen and they can't pay it back. I saw what happened to them.

I had loved ones in gangs so I seen what happens when fakers violate the rules. I know what would happen if I misrepresented my neighborhood, Highland. I accepted all the consequences that came with any decision I ever made. But I made sure it was something I know I could handle.

This is what I want my kids and grandkids to understand: before you do anything in life, you need to understand the consequences. Don't go back and forth with people unless they have just as much to lose as you. And stay away from people who don't have nothing to lose at all.

The system will tear a black family apart like it's nothing. I come from a long line of hustlers and players. Some stood tall, but some turned out to be very small. I still appreciate those guys in Highland who stand on what HPH is supposed to be about: family. Inside the home or outside—I always had someone with major street ties telling me the consequences of trying to get over in these streets. It can be cold, but its fair. I can honestly say, nobody ever encouraged me to sell dope, join a gang, or pimp women, even if they were doing those things themselves. They told me: listen to your mom, stay in school, don't be like us.

This was Highland, so I could never be too sure why some of the coldest hustlers, and gangsters in the city would tell me to stay out of the streets. They probably only told me because they didn't want me trying to get in, potentially cutting into their money. They knew I would never come in as just a worker for them, so warning me was probably their way of protecting what they had as well. They knew I had access to a solid plug if I didn't have nothing else. But they also knew my plug wasn't trying to put me in the game before I was ready anyway.

None the less, because I knew the consequences, I only had one foot in the streets instead of both when I was out there. Depending on who is talking about me, some might say I did have both feet in the game, and I was balling. Others might say I didn't do anything. It's all perspectives and opinions. Depending on who's talking about me, I never felt the need to confirm or deny anything a hater say about me. let them think whatever they want to think about me as long as they stay away from me.

The fact is: I lived the street life for a long time. Long enough that if I wasn't moving smart, I would have caught some kind of case for sure. It's hard to come from Highland and not have no streetness or gangster about you. But at the end of the day, I'm just glad I never caught a case. I'm thankful I had family and friends around me who I could learn from. I learned from their mistakes, and I learned from their successes. It helped me when it was time for me to make my own moves.

All my life I had to think smart and move carefully. I don't mix and mingle with everybody. I know looks are deceiving, so I still don't trust nobody. I know that no matter how tough some of these guys appear to be in the streets they will snitch when they get jammed up. I know that no matter how fine I think a woman is, the police and the streets think she fine too. If somebody snatch her up, she will tell everything she knows or even make up something to tell if she's scared. If you don't think a lot of these girls out here are low-key informants, YOU A FOOL.

Men snitch and women snitch too. This is the reason I know it's best for me to stay out of everybody's way. When I started seeing dumb dudes getting access to real money, and I mean dudes who I know for a fact is literally dumb, I knew it was time for me to get out of the streets. Dumb, goofy, and reckless dudes don't deserve good plugs, and they don't deserve to get rich either. It must be the system behind that. It must be some kind of trap.

In the hood, when one d boy goes to jail, a junky will just find the next d boy up. When one connect goes to jail or gets murdered then it's on to the next plug or connect. If a pimp gets locked up, his woman chooses the next pimp. The game doesn't stop, because the system won't let it stop. Their prisons are made to stay full.

Knowing what's happening in the streets is one thing. Knowing there's an invisible hand stirring the pot is another. I know the division in my community isn't by accident. The system has invested decades of time, money, and resources to keep the streets under their control. They hedge bets that we'll stay divided—and they don't plan on losing. They spend millions making it look like they're doing all they can to fix things, while at the same time creating more division. And they know we don't have the same time, money, and resources to fight for our unity.

Debt, Dysfunction, and Division for all.

Throughout this book, I've unpacked the many systems that shape—and often destroy—Black lives in America: the justice system, the financial system, the education system, the employment system, the legal system, and even the street system. Each of these, while functioning independently on the surface, are still interconnected to form the complete system. Together, they form a web of control with limited outcomes for Black people: lose our minds, fall into addiction, be locked in jails or prisons, end up dead—or sell out for money.

The U.S. Constitution and its amendments were drafted by white men, for the benefit of white men. Even the so-called "Bill of Rights"—which promises freedoms of speech, religion, fair trials, and protection from unjust government action—was written during a time when our ancestors were forced to work for free. These rights were not extended to us. They were written to serve as a framework for white liberty, not Black liberation.

It wasn't until the 13th, 14th, and 15th Amendments—passed only after the bloodshed of the Civil War—that the Constitution even began to acknowledge our humanity. The

13th abolished slavery "except as punishment for a crime," a loophole that laid the foundation for mass incarceration. The 14th was supposed to guarantee Black people equal protection under the law and citizenship rights. But from the jump, it was undermined by policies, court decisions, and violent resistance. The 15th gave us the right to vote—but not without voter suppression.

The 14th Amendment should have been our shield. This amendment was made FOR BLACK PEOPLE. It should have dismantled Jim Crow, protected us from state-sanctioned violence, and stopped discriminatory practices in housing, employment, and education. Unfortunately, the same system that wrote the law also controls how it's interpreted and enforced. So, while the language says, "equal protection," the lived reality remains anything but equal.

Other groups have tried to leap over black people and use the 14th Amendment for their own causes, and they have been successful with it. So, we see that justice is not blind—it just refuses to look our way. Its only so much being ignored people can take before they react and revolt against it. The system knows this too. But instead of working together to make things fair and equal, the system will bring in police, national guards, etc. etc. and form their weapons against us.

These people who run the government are so evil. They created the conditions for us to destroy ourselves. And while that plays out, they take the money generated by our destruction to upgrade their system: smarter surveillance, faster policing, more efficient oppression, social engineering, and A.I.

If this country ever hopes to live up to the promise of "liberty and justice for all," we must do more than reform the system—we must reimagine it. Dismantle it. Rebuild it with equity at its foundation and humanity at its core. The best way we can do this is get unified and stay out of prison over dumb stuff.

As a rapper from Milwaukee, I can't close out this book without naming another control system: record labels.

When I found hip hop, it saved my life. Hip hop was, at its best, a pure representation of creative expression—raw experiences from artists across the country, laid down in high-level, thought-provoking rhymes. Especially in the late 80's and all through the 90's, most of the respected artist were able to move the crowd with high level word play and lyricism. Those individuals who's vocabulary was too simple, too basic, too ignorant, or their writing was low-level, many listeners wouldn't take them seriously. Those artists were considered just rappers, not M.C.'s. There was levels to it, and to be respected as an M.C was a great thing. Hip Hop was controlled by the culture, not greedy white businessmen. This was in a time where the fans voices mattered. In the '90s, when tapes and CDs came with lyric booklets, I read every word like it was a novel. I wrote my first rhyme in Building 6, apartment 603. Listening to my favorite artists in my room and studying their albums kept me off the streets a lot. I loved writing raps so much it sharpened my own reading, writing, and comprehension skills.

At this time, it's the complete opposite. There are no levels to it, and almost no skills required. Most of the albums coming out are not worth studying. Unless you want to study the tragedy of how arrogant greedy executives came up with their own agenda to take over or destroy hip hop as a culture.

Nowadays, they give all the big marketing, promotional pushes, and attention to the simplest, most ignorant, and most non talented rappers. They shut down competition by spending additional millions paying media outlets and algorithms to ignore, silence and suppress truly talented artists who properly represent Black culture. If an artist is too talented, too conscious, or too pro black, they're seen as a threat—not to fans, but to label executives. Talented artists know their worth. Labels don't want that. They want young, hungry kids who'll sign their lives away because anything feels better than being broke. They prey on broken homes, financial illiteracy, and desperation.

Labels support rappers with no skill because the executives are arrogant and think they are the prize. They think that anybody they put in front of their cameras should be grateful to them. They sign individuals who are ok with being their pawns. They accept whatever deals they are given, no matter if part of it is about reinforcing white media's desired image of Blackness—loud, violent, hypersexual, and criminal.

Once those artists gain popularity, the mission is accomplished: That is the record labels return on investment. The rapper becomes an influence, put on display for ignorant behavior, and an entire younger generation is pushed to think that individual is cool, and to want to be like that.

The executives who run these labels aren't invested in culture; they're invested in control. They spend millions promoting the youngest, most ignorant, uneducated individuals, then parade them as "rappers." Their ego makes them think they can make anyone famous. It's true because they can push their individual to the top of algorithms for a little money while spending millions to silence and suppress artists who actually reflect Black culture in a positive and more authentic way. To them, it's not about talent or truth. It's about ownership, ego and control.

Like Jerry Jones owning the Dallas Cowboys, these executives want all the praise and credit. They would rather sign untalented individuals then talented artists who know their worth. These executives believe they deserve the right to have a say so in Black culture because they own the platforms and labels. They will spend just as much money to block and suppress talented artists, as they spend on signing naïve individuals who just want fame and attention. The label probably gets all the money back through the bad deals they give to individuals. They primarily target the non-talented, non-business minded, non-culturally aware, non-threat individuals, because these individuals will end up owing the record company anyway. This gives the record companies extra money to spend on blocking, suppressing, and shadow banning talented artist. They will spend millions to make sure not too many conscious or woke rappers get in any positions to create a real cultural movement. This is how they destroy the culture. They spend money to make the sellouts and ignorant minded individuals rich and famous because its better for the system that way. They will spend even more money, time, and resources to block the real talented artists.

This is no accident. The system will go to whatever lengths to push the narrative that education, discipline, and doing things the right way is "corny" or "played out." Young people are being sold the lie that if you're not rich, ignorant, and flashy before 25, you're not cool.

For young women, the trap is different but just as dangerous. The system promotes the hypersexualized, attention-chasing image as the standard. They want girls to idolize influencers and strippers over doctors, lawyers, or virtuous women. The agenda is clear: sell the idea that ratchet behavior is cool, and bury the truth that intelligence, character, and class is what its really about.

It's all intentional. Billions are invested—not to uplift—but to keep Black communities divided, distracted, and misinformed and imprisoned.

But here's the kicker:
these devils think they run they yard, but they are the prisoners.

Slavery is their prison.
The stain of being legacy slave owners and architects of oppression will never wash away.

Jim Crow is their prison.
Their laws and policies mark them forever as dehumanizers.

Discrimination is their prison.
They're trapped in a mindset that weaponizes privilege instead of building equality.

Racism is their prison.
Their fear and hatred of difference is a cage they can't escape.

Debt is their prison.
With the U.S. buried under $36 trillion, their "leadership" has produced nothing but division and dysfunction.

In Wisconsin, one in every 36 Black adults is incarcerated. At the same time, America sits in $36 trillion of debt. That's their scoreboard: prisons full of Black bodies, and a country bankrupt in every way that matters.

Dr. Claude Anderson has estimated that Black Americans are owed $14 trillion in reparations. Yet the wicked can't pay their debts because they are spiritually bankrupt. They are too consumed with holding onto white privilege to recognize their own imprisonment. They set traps for us but ended up locking themselves in.

So while they waste energy trying to control our culture, I'll keep knowing my rights and enjoying my freedom. Black people will keep elevating, innovating, and creating new things. The oppressors will remain locked in the prisons they keep trying to create for our people.

Craig Brown

*

Never Caught A Case

Song lyrics from the album Social Just'Us (2018)

Social Just'Us Album original design made by me(2018)

Craig Brown

Never Caught A Case (Song Lyrics)

-Man I ain't Never caught a case
A Black man in the United States
(That's incredible, truly incredible)

-Man I ain't never caught a case
(Ay we gone pop bottles to this
Pop, bottles to this)

-Cuz I ain't never caught a case
-I hope you never catch a case

(1st Verse)
-So many nights my momma prayed for my safety,
I'm her youngest son
She ain't want the streets to take me.
-I learned from the best hustlers
I wasn't shaky,
I jumped off the porch
3 grams for the $80.
-My 1st spot on Kilbourn
This cool old lady,
She let me use her crib
let me know where all the J's be.
-She had so many roaches in her crib
it was CRAZY,
but I still ran up $500 every day.
-That house was so nasty
All I could think about was hustlin,
Wouldn't sit on nuthin,
Wouldn't touch nuthin,
Wouldn't eat nuthin,
-Dusted and disgusted

still I had to run it up,
wanted to show my older brothers how I was really cut.
-Get it out the mud
straight getting it how I live
and I wasn't the only D boy serving out her crib.
-Crazy thing
after I left and found a new spot,
I heard It got hot
feds raided
came and boarded up the whole block.
-Them streets never had me shook though
I didn't stop,
I was on to the next
get some more guap.
-Like Lonzo's pops I had to Ball,
but hustlin wasn't top priority to me
I wasn't greedy so.

(Chorus)
-I never caught a case.
A Black man in the United States
and
-I ain't never caught a case.
And I ain't never had to rat
Just stack and
-I ain't never caught a case.
(Aye we gone pop bottles to this)
So many real ones done got caught up in the trap
-but I ain't never caught a case.
(Free the real ones)
I hope u never catch a case.

(Verse 2)
-I don't know why they call the game The game,

Ain't nobody playing but these lames
-These lames. Make it bad for everybody
they in the way mane.
cuz they ain't doing it for the paper they doing it for
the fame.
-I worked hard to make sure my name ain't out there
In these streets
where people in ya business like welfare.
-I was smart enough to
get that white clientele
they had more to lose than me so all is well.
-Kept me a 9-5 gig
and it paid well
still in the hood
but I was livin like fresh prince of Belair.
-My big bro caught a case
that was my worse nightmare
but he knew more about them streets than I did
from in there.
-Words of wisdom & game shared
on every conversation
Who got murked
Who snitchin
Who not to trust Who hating.
-Who bossed up Who out the game Who faking
I wouldn't tell you you should do it
but I can tell you how I did it
and

(Chorus)
-I ain't never caught a case.
A Black man in the United States and
-I ain't never caught a case.
And I ain't never had to rat

Never Caught A Case

Just stack
And I ain't never caught a case.
(Aye where them non alcoholic bottles at?)
-So many real ones done got caught up
In the trap
but I ain't never caught a case.
(Bless the real)
I hope u never catch a case
(You know that system prejudice man.)

(Bridge)
-Been in shootouts before,
I'm what you bout and more
-Raised with killers
Ran with hustlers
Never ran my mouth before.
-Been arrested, been sweated,
feds ran in my house before
-Don't nothing make you mad
Like seeing moms handcuffed on the floor.
-But I ain't never been to jail bruh
Never snitched
Never had to talk to 12 bruh
-Played them streets
Very well bruh
Stacked paper
And I ain't never caught a case.

Written by Craig Brown (2018) Social Just'Us Album.

Craig Brown

Acknowledgments

Thank God for allowing me to write this book.

To my children — Marcel Peters, Infinity Brown, Jordyn Brown — and to my grandchildren — Zailyn Wells, Kion Brown, A'Zari Brown, Josiah Price, and Eden Brown.

To Toni Janae Momon and Tamira.

To my big bro's DB, Ty, Stan, and my sister Kat.

Each of you inspired me to write this book in your own way. Shout out to all my relatives in Milwaukee, Chicago, and Mississippi. and shout out to HPH and the whole 414.

My Inspiration

My Inspiration

Craig Brown

*